ISSUES ASSOCIATED WITH THE IMPLEMENTATION OF ARTICLE 82 OF THE UNITED NATIONS CONVENTION ON THE LAW OF THE SEA

ISA TECHNICAL STUDY SERIES

Technical Study No. 1

Global Non-Living Resources on the Extended Continental Shelf: Prospects at the year 2000.

Technical Study No. 2

Polymetallic Massive Sulphides and Cobalt-Rich Ferromanganese Crusts: Status and Prospects.

Technical Study No. 3

Biodiversity, Species Ranges and Gene Flow in the Abyssal Pacific Nodule Province: Predicting and Managing the Impacts of Deep Seabed Mining.

ISSUES ASSOCIATED WITH THE IMPLEMENTATION OF ARTICLE 82 OF THE UNITED NATIONS CONVENTION ON THE LAW OF THE SEA

ISA TECHNICAL STUDY: NO. 4

International Seabed Authority
Kingston, Jamaica

National Library of Jamaica Cataloguing-in-Publication Data

International Seabed Authority
  Issues associated with the implementation of Article 82 of the United Nations Convention on the Law of the Sea.
      p. ; ill., map;   cm. – (ISA technical study; no.4)
      Includes bibliography
      ISBN: 978-976-95217-7-3
      1. Law of the sea 2. Ocean mining - Economic aspects 3. Ocean botton - Laws and legislation
      I. Title   II. Series
       341.448 – dc 21

International Seabed Authority
14–20 Port Royal Street
Kingston, Jamaica
Tel: (876) 9229105, Fax: (876) 9220195
URL: http://www.isa.org.jm

TABLE OF CONTENTS

LIST OF ABBREVIATIONS

AIPN	Association of International Petroleum Negotiators
Area (the)	International Seabed Area
Authority (the)	International Seabed Authority (also ISA)
C-NLOPB	Canada-Newfoundland and Labrador Offshore Petroleum Board
CLCS	Commission on the Limits of the Continental Shelf
EEZ	Exclusive Economic Zone
GDP	Gross Domestic Product
GNI	Gross National Income
HDI	Human Development Index
HPI	Human Poverty Index
ICJ	International Court of Justice
ICNT	Informal Composite Negotiating Text
ICOM	Integrated Coastal and Ocean Management
ILA	International Law Association
IOPCF	International Oil Pollution Compensation Fund
ISA	International Seabed Authority (also the Authority)
ISNT	Informal Single Negotiating Text
ITLOS	International Tribunal for the Law of the Sea
LOS Convention	United Nations Convention on the Law of the Sea, 1982
M	Nautical mile
MDG	Millennium Development Goals
MMS	Minerals Management Service (United States Department of the Interior)
MRM	Minerals Revenue Management, Minerals Management Service (United States Department of the Interior)
OCS	Outer continental shelf (or shelves)
ODA	Official Development Assistance
PrepCom	Preparatory Commission for the International Seabed Authority and for the International Tribunal for the Law of the Sea established under Annex 1 of the United Nations Convention on the Law of the Sea, 1982
RIK	Royalty-in-Kind
RSNT	Revised Single Negotiating Text
SPLOS	States Parties to the LOS Convention
UN	United Nations Organization
UNCLOS III	Third United Nations Conference on the Law of the Sea
US	United States of America
Vienna Convention	Vienna Convention on the Law of Treaties, 1969
WDI	World Development Indicators

LIST OF TEXT BOX, FIGURE AND TABLES

FOREWORD

The 1982 UN Convention on the Law of the Sea (the Convention) is the most important international regime governing the oceans. It covers a wide range of issues, including navigational rights, protection of the marine environment and, relevant for this paper, jurisdiction over living and non-living marine resources. The Convention entered into force in 1994 and, as of October 2009, 158 States and the European Community were parties to the Convention. Of the major powers, only the United States has yet to accede to the Convention, though there are indications it may soon join as well.

The negotiations leading up to the adoption of the Convention were long and complex. One particularly debated topic was the extent of a coastal State's continental shelf. This was eventually set at up to 200 nautical miles from its coastline. However, through a complex assessment mechanism the continental shelf can be extended up to a total of 350 nautical miles from the coastline if the coastal State can show that '*the natural prolongation of its submerged land territory to the outer edge of its continental margin extends beyond the 200-nautical-mile distance criterion.*' The area between the 200 nautical miles limit and the border of the total claim is called the Outer Continental Shelf (OCS).

The resources that occur on the world's continental margins may include oil, natural gas, gas hydrates, manganese nodules, sand, gravel, titanium, thorium, iron, nickel, copper, cobalt, gold and diamonds. The size and value of these deposits is unknown, but potential OCS claims cover a large section of the seabed. For comparison, OCS claims could be in excess of 15 million square kilometres, while the world's exclusive economic zones (the water column within 200 nautical miles of the coast) are estimated at approximately 85 million square kilometres, and the Area consists of around 260 million square kilometres.

According to the provisions of the Convention, States wishing to claim an OCS, are required to submit particulars of the claim within ten years of the date of their ratification of the Convention. Because of the difficulty for many States that had ratified the Convention several years ago in complying with that deadline, the Meeting of States Parties to the Convention had agreed that States that ratified the Convention before 13 May 1999 would be permitted to submit their claims by 13 May 2009. As of that date, 51 full submissions to OCS areas and 44 preliminary submissions had been made by more than 70 States. Only about fifteen of these States do not have developing-country status. For many of these developing nations, the added areas of seabed could be economically critical. In particular, land-poor countries such as Barbados, Tonga and Palau are hoping to help secure their financial future with underwater resources.

Sections of the ocean floor that are not part of a territorial claim are called the Area. The mineral resources of the Area are considered a common heritage of mankind and, as a result, those who exploit it have to pay fees for their licences and activities in the Area. That revenue is globally apportioned, with particular emphasis on the needs of developing countries and land-locked States (since the latter have no other way to benefit from marine resources). The International Seabed Authority (the Authority), an intergovernmental organization established by the Convention, was specifically established to act on behalf of humankind in the Area and is tasked with the organization and control of activities in the Area.

The potential extension of coastal States' continental shelves to 350 nautical miles erodes the size of the Area – and hence the resources available to developing and land-locked States. Article 82 of the Convention, which is the subject matter of the present technical study, was introduced as a quid pro quo for this. Article 82 is a unique provision in international law. Motivated by a sense of fairness, it establishes an international 'servitude' in the form of a 'royalty' consisting of payments and contributions to be made by the coastal State to the Authority for the exploitation of the non-living resources of the OCS. There are very few, if any, similar provisions in any other legal instrument which set out a legal obligation designed to address international inequity in a practical way, not simply as a political aspiration or in vague general terms. However Article 82 carries many ambiguities and uncertainties, in part because of its novelty, the difficult compromise behind it and unanswered questions about the mechanisms of implementation.

Responsibility for the implementation of Article 82 rests with the Authority and with States that exploit the non-living resources of their OCS. Payments and contributions are to be made annually by the OCS State at the rate of 1% on the value or volume of all production, commencing on the sixth year of production, increasing by 1% per year until the rate reaches 7% by the twelfth year, and thereafter remaining at 7%. The Authority then disburses those payments and contributions to State parties 'on the basis of equitable sharing criteria, taking into account the interests and needs of developing States, particularly the least developed and the land-locked among them.'

Although Article 82 has been dormant since the adoption of the Convention, there are coastal States, in particular Canada (which is a State Party to the Convention) and the United States (which is not yet), that have granted prospecting and/or exploration licences or leases on their OCS. Typically, offshore petroleum and mineral development operates on a timeframe that can span decades. Today's prospecting and exploration licence may become a development and production licence within perhaps 10–20 years of initial activity. However, it is possible that Article 82 revenues will come due as soon as 2015. Either way, Article 82 will soon awaken.

However, Article 82 is also a complex provision. It is also the only provision in the Convention setting out an international royalty concerning an activity *within* national jurisdiction. It contains a rough and untested formula to determine payments or contributions. The uniqueness and complexity of Article 82 demand careful consideration of the obligation, principles and criteria for distribution of benefits, procedural aspects, the role of the Authority, the role of OCS States, and economic and temporal issues.

The Convention provides little guidance to the Authority on how Article 82 might be implemented. Accordingly, one major issue for the Authority is to determine the full extent of its mandate and related powers and functions as it discharges its Article

82 responsibilities. For example, the Council (the executive organ of the Authority comprising 36 elected States) is tasked with recommending to the Assembly (the political body of all 159 members) rules, regulations and procedures on the equitable sharing of financial and other economic benefits made by virtue of Article 82, taking into account the interest and needs of developing States and peoples who have not attained full independence. However, the Article 82 text concerning distribution of payments and contributions suffers from ambiguity. Presumably 'taking into account' implies preferential consideration. What may be intended by 'interests and needs,' and according to whom, is not clear. For example, are developing States with basic livelihood needs on a par with developing States that wish to reduce their dependence on imported energy? Drawing upon existing indices, the Authority may need to develop another composite hierarchy of needs index to rank potential beneficiary States and peoples with reference to the objects and purposes of Article 82.

To begin to answer these, and other, questions around the interpretation and application of Article 82, the Authority, in conjunction with the Energy, Environment and Development Programme of the Royal Institute of International Affairs (Chatham House) in the United Kingdom, convened a seminar for a group of invited experts to discuss the issues associated with Article 82. Chatham House is one of the world's leading organizations for the analysis of international issues. It is membership-based and aims to help individuals and organizations to be at the forefront of developments in an ever-changing and increasingly complex world. The seminar was hosted by Chatham House in London from 11 – 13 February 2009. It was attended by a broad selection of leading academic and practitioner experts in the international law of the sea, marine geology and oceanography, as well as the offshore oil and gas industry from Europe, Africa, Asia, and North and South America (the list of participants appears in Annex IV).

Discussions at the seminar were assisted by two working papers commissioned by the Authority. The first paper, prepared by Dr Aldo Chircop of Dalhousie University, Canada, presented a study of issues associated with the implementation of Article 82 from a legal and policy perspective. The second paper, prepared by Dr Lindsay Parson of the National Oceanography Centre, Southampton, UK, provided a technical overview of the current status of OCS claims and the resource potential of OCS areas.

The present report is a revised version of Dr Chircop's paper. Following the seminar, the paper was extensively revised to take into account the views expressed by participants in the seminar and to try to reflect the thoughts of participants as to the way forward in addressing Article 82 issues. The Authority is extremely grateful to Dr Chircop not only for his original report, but also for the many hours spent in working with the legal staff of the Authority in revising the document in light of the discussions at Chatham House. In accordance with the Chatham House Rule, none of the views expressed at the seminar are attributed in this report to any particular individual or organization, including the Authority. The report is intended to have no status other than as a transparent and exhaustive study of the issues associated with the implementation of Article 82, compiled with the benefit of the views of some of the very best experts available, and potential suggestions for dealing with the most immediate issues.

The associated technical report by Dr Parson will also be published as a technical study by the Authority in due course.

The key recommendation of this report is that the Authority will need to develop a strategy for bringing Article 82 to the attention of Member States and to explore a practical approach for the implementation of Article 82. This is most easily, and appropriately, done while the provision is still dormant, especially as its implementation has both international and domestic implications. At this time, the discussion and resolution are more likely to be viewed as a technical than a political exercise. OCS States also face a range of challenges in implementing Article 82 and these should be addressed as soon as possible in order to promote consistency and certainty in State practice.

The Authority's work in relation to Article 82 is just beginning. Already, at the fifteenth session of the Authority, held in Kingston, Jamaica, in May 2009, Member States expressed interest in the outcomes of the Chatham House seminar and requested the Secretary-General to consider including matters relating to the implementation of Article 82 in the next programme of work for the Authority. It is hoped that the present report will provide a solid basis for Member States, whether OCS States or potential beneficiary States, to embark upon what is likely to be a long and detailed discussion of all the issues associated with Article 82 and its implementation.

Finally, the Authority wishes to express its appreciation to Chatham House and in particular Bernice Lee, Duncan Brack and the staff of the Energy, Environment and Development Programme, for their cooperation and enthusiasm for this project.

EXECUTIVE SUMMARY

The essence of Article 82

- Article 82 of the United Nations Convention on the Law of the Sea, 1982 (LOS Convention) stipulates an obligation on States Parties to make payments or contributions in kind with respect to the exploitation of the non-living resources of their outer continental shelves (OCS). Developing States that are net importers of the mineral resource produced on their OCS are exempt from this obligation in relation to that mineral resource.

- Payments and contributions are to be made annually at the rate of one percent on the value or volume of all production, commencing on the sixth year of production, and increasing by one percent per year until the rate reaches seven percent on the twelfth year, and thereafter remaining at seven percent. Resources used in connection with exploitation are not considered part of production.

- The payments or contributions are made by the coastal State through the International Seabed Authority (the Authority), an inter-governmental organization established by the LOS Convention with respect to activities in the International Seabed Area (the Area). The Authority is tasked to distribute the payments and contributions to States Parties in accordance with equitable criteria, taking into account the interests and needs of developing States, and in particular the least developed and land-locked States, and peoples who have not yet achieved full independence or other self-governing status.

Status and responsibility for implementation

- Although Article 82 is a dormant provision (i.e., it has not been implemented to date), there are coastal States which have granted prospecting and/or exploration licences or leases on their OCS. As coastal States proceed to define the outer limits of their continental shelves in accordance with Article 76 and following recommendations from the Commission on the Limits of the Continental Shelf, there will be an increase of OCS areas that will potentially fall within the ambit of Article 82.

- Article 82 establishes a unique international royalty on non-living resource exploitation. It was negotiated into the LOS Convention during the Third United

Nations Conference on the Law of the Sea (UNCLOS III) as a *quid pro quo* for the coastal State's right in Article 76 to define the outer limit of its continental shelf to encompass continental margin areas outside the 200-nautical mile limit.

• Responsibility for the implementation of Article 82 rests with States that exploit the non-living resources of their OCS and the Authority. The LOS Convention provides powers and functions to the Assembly and Council to enable the Authority to perform its responsibilities.

Context for interpretation

• Article 82 has several textual ambiguities and gaps raising questions that require clarification. There is need for interpretation of explicit stipulations and for inferences of implicit requirements to facilitate practical implementation. As a treaty provision, Article 82 requires interpretation against the international law of treaties, the overall text of the LOS Convention as the package deal of which it is an integral part, the negotiation history and process of UNCLOS III and the backdrop of the contemporary context of implementation.

Issues for OCS States

• OCS States are exempted from making payments or contributions during the first five years of production (i.e., the grace period). OCS States will need to determine commercial viability of deep-water drilling against the backdrop of Article 82.

• The OCS States have the option of making either payments (e.g., in monies) or contributions in kind. The LOS Convention does not indicate a procedure for the determination of the precise amount of payment or in-kind contribution, and the Authority has not been given an assessment power in this regard. Nor does the LOS Convention indicate whether the OCS State can change its choice of payments or contributions in kind after it has already commenced discharging the obligation.

• The meaning of "value" for the purposes of calculating the applicable percentage will need to be clarified for the non-living resource concerned. This could refer to the well-head value in the case of hydrocarbons, i.e., when the product is brought to the surface, but before transportation. The applicable year will need to be determined (e.g., type of calendar year and/or fiscal year) for the OCS State and the Authority. In relation to payments, the LOS Convention does not stipulate a rule on currency, but given the purpose of the payments and contributions to benefit other States, an international or widely-used currency could be implied. Also, the OCS State is not permitted to deduct the costs associated with the making of payments and contributions.

• OCS States should inform themselves of the implications of Article 82 for offshore development. In particular, as early as during the planning of royalty regimes and granting of exploration licences on the OCS, the domestic implementation needs should be considered.

Issues for the Authority

- The Authority will need to assist its Member States to better understand the full extent of its mandate, implementation needs and related powers and functions to discharge its Article 82 responsibilities. The Council is tasked with recommending to the Assembly the rules, regulations and procedures on the equitable sharing of financial and other economic benefits made by virtue of Article 82, taking into account the interests and needs of developing States and peoples who have not attained full independence. The Assembly will consider the recommendations and if it does not agree with them may refer them back to the Council.

- For the Authority to discharge its responsibilities, it is likely that it will need to further develop its institutional capacities. Cooperation with OCS States will be essential. The Authority will need periodic communication with and information from producing OCS States. The Authority needs to be informed of: the date of commencement of production; the nature of the non-living resource exploited; the location of the resource; the form of discharge of the obligation by OCS States (i.e., whether by payments or contributions) and related matters that would enable it to receive and pass on the benefits to beneficiaries. A potential issue is commercially sensitive information which the OCS might wish to protect, but which the Authority might need to discharge its tasks.

- The Authority can be expected to incur expenses in discharging its Article 82 tasks. In particular, when contributions in kind are made, the Authority might conceivably incur costs in receiving or transporting or holding the contribution until it is passed on to beneficiaries. The bare text of the LOS Convention does not provide for the Authority to recover its expenses from the payments and contributions before they are passed on to beneficiaries. It will likely be essential for Member States to consider how the costs of the administration of Article 82 might be covered. An interpretation of Article 82 in this regard might be needed.

- The LOS Convention does not provide guidance on the ultimate application of distributed payments and contributions to beneficiaries. Taking into consideration the fact that the prioritized beneficiaries of Article 82 payments are developing States, the overall purpose appears to be developmental. There are several potential avenues for the distribution of Article 82 benefits including: the development of a novel distribution process within the Authority; the utilization of reputable existing international and regional mechanisms and linking with the Kyoto Protocol Adaptation Fund.

- The Authority is required to develop equitable criteria for the distribution of payments and contributions to States Parties. It is unclear whether equitable criteria for the distribution of Part XI economic and financial benefits, which have as yet to be developed, may be the same as for Article 82. The development of equitable criteria may need to occur in the modern context of the Millennium Development Goals and multiple human and economic development indices maintained by international organizations, in particular the United Nations Development Programme and the World Bank. Drawing upon existing indices, the Authority may need to develop its own composite index to rank potential beneficiary States and peoples, as may be appropriate, with reference to the objects and purposes of the LOS Convention.

Implementation tasks

• Both OCS States and the Authority have several issues to resolve in order to discharge their respective implementation responsibilities. Given the long temporal scope of offshore non-living resource exploration and exploitation and the expectations set out in Article 82, it is advisable for OCS States and the Authority to approach implementation demands in a phased manner. The anticipated phases of the implementation tasks, which are set out in this report with respect to OCS States and the Authority, could be as follows:

    • Phase 1: A pre-production period covering the stage of prospecting, exploration and development of licences or leases, but before commencement of commercial production. In this phase OCS States and the Authority would begin to anticipate the administrative and fiscal consequences of the OCS royalty.

    • Phase 2: A grace period covering the first five years of OCS royalty-free production. This would be a transitional period during which the producer would be expected to recover costs. The OCS State would enjoy a royalty-free period and the Authority would be putting procedures in place for receiving payments and contributions in kind and for their distribution.

    • Phase 3: The OCS royalty period when payments and contributions in kind would be expected to commence with the sixth year of production and, according to the rising scale identified earlier, the Authority would distribute the benefits to beneficiaries on an ongoing basis. This period would be co-extensive with the commercial life of the non-living resource exploited.

• Given the likely long-term relationship between producing OCS States and the Authority, as well as the uncertainties identified in this report, it is advisable for a producing OCS State and the Authority to enter into an Article 82 agreement. For this purpose, and in anticipation of the operationalization of Article 82, it is advisable that the OCS States and the Authority formulate a "Model Article 82 Agreement," within the framework of the LOS Convention, and upon which Authority/OCS State-specific agreements would be entered into in the future. Such an agreement would perform the function of an OCS royalty agreement and be the basis upon which the respective responsibilities in Article 82 (insofar as the making and handling of payments and contributions are concerned) can be coordinated and administered. It is advisable for the Authority to take the lead in developing such a model agreement, in close cooperation with experts from OCS States and other States Parties of the LOS Convention.

- A concern for Article 82 implementation is a hypothetical scenario of non-living resources straddling the limits of the OCS. Article 82 applies only to production from the non-living resources of the OCS and, in the case of a unitized development, the cooperating States concerned would need to agree on the respective shares of production, which will then serve as a basis for computing payments and contributions in kind. More complex is the situation where the resource straddles the Area where the OCS State, and/or contractor concerned, would need to cooperate with the Authority or its designate.

Dispute resolution

- OCS States are required by general international law and the LOS Convention to fulfill their obligations under the Convention in good faith and not to exercise their rights in a manner which amounts to an abuse of the rights of others. Given the uncertainties in Article 82, this general duty can be expected to play an important role in the implementation of Article 82.

- Should there be disputes between OCS States and the Authority, or for that matter other States Parties to the LOS Convention, the Convention's Part XV dispute settlement regime does not provide a compulsory mechanism for the resolution of such disputes. It is likely that the Authority may not be able to resolve such disputes through the Seabed Disputes Chamber, because Article 82 disputes do not concern activities in the Area.

- The Council and/or Assembly may be in a position to seek an advisory opinion on the legal interpretation of the provision from the Seabed Disputes Chamber, although this will not be conclusive.

- An alternative solution is for another State Party to resort to Part XV procedures to resolve an issue concerning the interpretation or application of Article 82.

- It may also be useful for ITLOS to anticipate the demands of Article 82 disputes and convene a seminar involving Tribunal judges to explore how the dispute settlement framework in the LOS Convention might be of assistance to States Parties in resolving such disputes.

Next steps for the Authority

- Should the Authority decide to proceed with an implementation strategy for its responsibilities regarding Article 82, the following steps should be considered for inclusion in the strategy:

- The first step is to introduce the subject to Member States. Article 82 could be brought to the attention of Member States in the Secretary-General's Annual Report by way of a short explanation of the provision and the practical issues of implementation that it entails.
- Member States should be invited to consider including the question of the future implementation of Article 82 in the Authority's programme of work: in the first instance, this may be through a meeting of a group of experts.
- Upon inclusion in the programme of work, the Legal and Technical Commission should commence consideration of the Authority's implementation responsibilities and eventually forward to the Council appropriate recommendations for the establishment of rules, regulations and procedures. An expert group meeting, including members of the Commission, may provide a useful starting point for such consideration.
- The Authority needs to start considering the development of an arrangement with OCS States, as key actors in giving effect to Article 82. The development of implementation guidelines to assist the governments of the numerous OCS States potentially affected by Article 82 should be considered.
- The equitable distribution of payments and contributions needs a well-developed framework, process and criteria. The Authority should convene a workshop of experts from Member States to consider practical options for further consideration by the Legal and Technical Commission.
- On the advice of the Legal and Technical Commission, the Council will need to propose to the Assembly the rules, regulations and procedures on equitable sharing of Article 82 benefits.

1. INTRODUCTION

Article 82 of the *United Nations Convention on the Law of the Sea*, 1982 (LOS Convention or the Convention) is a unique provision in international law.[1] Article 82 is motivated by a sense of international equity.[2] It establishes an international "royalty" consisting of payments and contributions on the exploitation of the non-living resources of the outer continental shelf (OCS). The OCS is that part of the continental shelf which extends beyond 200 nautical miles (M) from the baselines of the territorial sea. It is the only provision in the LOS Convention setting out an international royalty concerning an activity *within* national jurisdiction. In comparison, deep-seabed miners have to pay to the International Seabed Authority (the Authority) administrative fees for their licences and activities in the international seabed area (the Area) and eventually a royalty on the mining of mineral resources.[3]

This provision has been dormant since the adoption of the LOS Convention. It is one of the few provisions of the LOS Convention for which few, if any, steps towards its implementation have been taken by potentially affected OCS States and the Authority. Recent international commercial and domestic regulatory interest on non-living resources in deep-water areas of the OCS have raised the distinct possibility that this provision may soon be coming of age. It is likely that the Authority, as the competent international institution to administer Article 82 payments and contributions, will be expected to anticipate and take steps towards the implementation of this provision, a responsibility that it shares with other States Parties to the LOS Convention, and in particular the OCS States.

Article 82 is both a specific bargain and an integral part of a larger package deal. Although a unique provision, it was not negotiated on its own at the Third United Nations Conference on the Law of the Sea (UNCLOS III). Rather, its negotiation was an integral part of the negotiations concerning the Article 76 entitlement to an outer continental shelf. In principle and spirit, Article 82 is the *quid pro quo* for the re-definition of the continental shelf to encompass the continental margin, with the effect of reducing the

---

[1] *United Nations Convention on the Law of the Sea*, Montego Bay, 10 December 1982 (in force: 16 November 1994), 1833 UNTS 3 [hereafter the LOS Convention]. A consolidated version of the LOS Convention and other accompanying basic texts are reproduced in *The Law of the Sea: Compendium of Basic Documents* (Kingston, Jamaica: International Seabed Authority & Caribbean Law Publishing Co., 2001) [hereafter Compendium].

[2] Tommy T. B. Koh, Ambassador of Singapore and President of UNCLOS III, "A Constitution for the Oceans," in Compendium, ibid., lx–lxiv, at lxi.

[3] See Resolution II Governing Preparatory Investment in Pioneer Activities Relating to Polymetallic Nodules, Final Act of the Third United Nations Conference on the Law of the Sea, Montego Bay, 10 December 1982, in Compendium, ibid., 325–332.

size of the Area. A coastal State's entitlement to Article 76 outer continental shelf benefits is "conditioned" by the obligation in Article 82. The LOS Convention does not permit States Parties to make any exceptions or reservations.[4] At the end of UNCLOS III, the general sentiment among the delegations at UNCLOS III was that the provisions of the LOS Convention are indivisible.[5]

Article 82 is also a complex provision. It contains a rough and untested formula to determine payments or contributions with respect to the exploitation of the non-living resources of the OCS. The uniqueness and complexity of Article 82 demand careful consideration of the substantive obligation, principles and criteria for distribution of benefits, procedural aspects, role of the Authority, and economic and temporal issues while the provision is still "dormant." The implementation of Article 82 has both international and domestic implications.

Against this backdrop, this report consists of an "issues paper" that attempts to identify challenges and steps to facilitate implementation of this provision.

---

[4] Unless specifically permitted by a particular provision in the Convention. LOS Convention, supra note 1, Art. 309.

[5] "The second theme which emerged from the statements [made by delegations at Montego Bay in December 1982] is that the provisions of the Convention are closely interrelated and form an integral package. Thus it is not possible for a State to pick what it likes and to disregard what it does not like. It was also said that rights and obligations go hand in hand and it is not permissible to claim rights under the Convention without being willing to shoulder the corresponding obligations." Koh, in Compendium, supra note 1, at lxi. Traditional treaty interpretation and application theory supports this view. See Lord McNair, *The Law of Treaties* (Oxford: Clarendon Press, 1961), 484.

2. STATUS AND PROSPECTS OF RESOURCE EXPLOITATION ON THE OCS

Article 82 concerns production of non-living resources on the extended continental shelf. Extended continental shelves are known to contain a wide range of non-living resources which, while not in production at this time, carry future promise. Among promising resources are aggregates, evaporates, gas hydrates, hydrocarbons, manganese nodules and crusts, placers, phosphorites and polymetallic sulphides.

A separate report assessing the status and prospects of non-living resource exploitation on the OCS has been published by the Authority.[6] At the time of writing, North American States have their offshore prospecting and exploration licensing or leasing on the OCS, primarily for oil and gas. For example, Canada, a State Party, has already issued exploration licences on the OCS off Newfoundland and Labrador and more calls for bids have been issued recently (see Figure 1).[7] The United States, which is not a State Party to the LOS Convention, has also issued leases on the OCS in the Gulf of Mexico and other areas.[8] Discoveries have been made in seaward areas within exclusive economic zones (EEZs) in other parts of the world, suggesting that discoveries farther seaward of the EEZ limit are also possible. Other marine regions are known, or suspected, to have OCS mineral resource potential. Brazil's Santos Basin has recently attracted attention and deep water areas may well be interesting for new reserves.[9] A significant discovery has been made by the Italian state-owned company, Eni, in deep water offshore Angola.[10] Similarly, optimistic assessments have been made for other areas of West Africa.[11]

---

[6] *Non-living and living resources of the seafloor beyond 200 nautical miles and their significance for application of Article 82 of the United Nations Convention on the Law of the Sea*, ISA Technical study No. 5 (Kingston, Jamaica: International Seabed Authority, 2009).

[7] In particular, bids for C-NLOPB NLO8-1 (Central Ridge/Flemish Pass) for areas outside 200M (see Figure 1) have been accepted. The three parcels for this area generated just under CAD $40 million. See "C-NLOPB Receives 5 Exploration Bids Offshore Newfoundland, Labrador," C-NLOPB 17 November 2008, http://www.rigzone.com/news/article.asp?a_id=69563.

[8] Note that in US law the "outer continental shelf" has a different meaning from the use of the term in the international law of the sea. The Minerals Management Service (MMS) defines this as "the submerged lands, subsoil, and seabed, lying between the States' seaward jurisdiction and the seaward extent of Federal jurisdiction," administered by the Federal Government. MMS, http://www.mms.gov/aboutmms/ocs.htm. The legal definition is provided in *Outer Continental Shelf Lands Act*, 43 U.S.C. § 1331 et seq; 43 U.S.C. § 1801 et seq. For a map of the 2007-2012 lease programme, see MMS, http://www.mms.gov/5-year/PDFs/ocs_status_map_8e.pdf.

[9] "Play potential in the deepwater Santos Basin," 68(9) *Offshore* (September 2008), http://www.offshore-mag.com/display_article/272394/120/ARTCL/none/none/1/Play-potential-in-the-deepwater-Santos-basin,-Brazil/.

[10] "Eni makes new oil discovery offshore Angola," Reuters Africa, 14 October 2008, http://africa.reuters.com/business/news/usnJOE49D0AB.html. See also "Eni starts ball rolling on new Angolan project," 10(21) *Deepwater International* 1 (20 October 2008).

[11] See "West Africa shows promise," 68(5) *Offshore* (1 May 2008), http://www.offshore-mag.com/articles/save_screen.cfm?ARTICLE_ID=329197.

FIGURE 1: EXPLORATION LICENCES ON CANADA'S OCS OFFSHORE NEWFOUNDLAND
& LABRADOR, NORTHWEST ATLANTIC

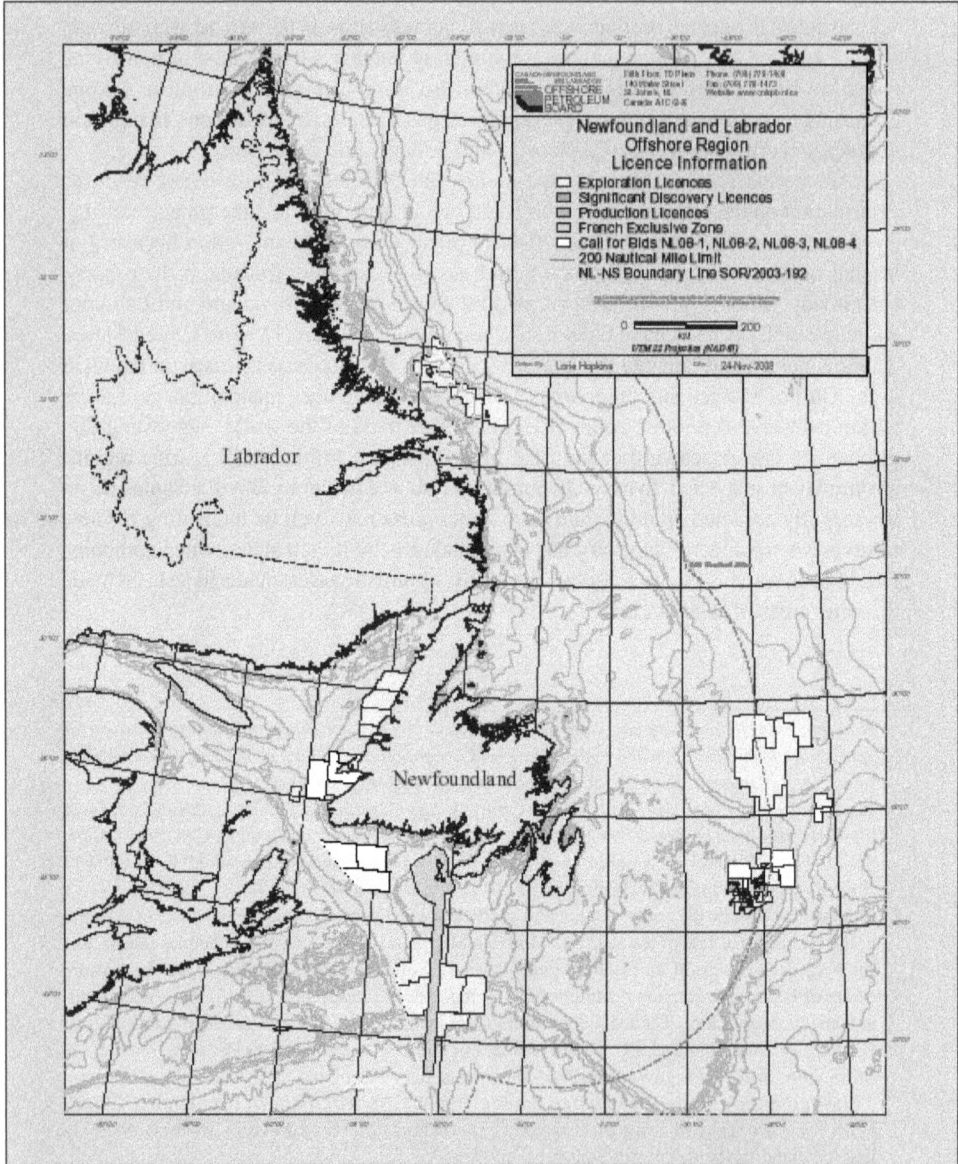

Source: Canada-Newfoundland & Labrador Offshore Petroleum Board (C-NOPB), 2008.
http://www.cnlopb.nl.ca/maps/onl_2008.pdf).

Typically, offshore petroleum and mineral development policies and contracting practices operate on long time frames that can span decades. Today's prospecting and exploration licence may become a development and production licence, perhaps between ten and 20 years from initial activity.[12] The production licence can be expected to last for 20 years or more. In general, the deeper the offshore activity, the more likely that costs will be higher and, consequently, the longer the period needed for cost-recovery. Depending on how the Article 82 obligation is implemented by OCS States, there will likely be a need for long-term planning within the time frames of the offshore petroleum and mineral industries. For example, if the OCS State intends to recover the value of the payment or contribution through its domestic royalty regime, it would need to undertake significant advance planning and consultation with holders of licences, and in some jurisdictions also with sub-national levels of government.

National authorities of States Parties concerned with the contemporary administration and regulation of offshore hydrocarbons and mineral exploration and development will need to consider the possibility that Article 82 will have a role to play in the event of discoveries leading to production on the OCS. The growing attention to and activities on OCS areas around the world and industry's time frame for operations highlight the importance of taking early steps to put in place a national framework for the implementation of Article 82. Although not a party to the LOS Convention, at the time of writing, the United States is probably the only State that formally alerted the offshore industry concerning Article 82 in calls for bids. Since at least 2001, and most recently at the time of writing in 2008, the Minerals Management Service (MMS, Department of the Interior) has advised lessees in successive rounds of leasing that contingent royalty payment provisions would apply if the United States becomes a party

---

[12] Time frames differ from one jurisdiction to another. For example in The Netherlands the offshore hydrocarbon exploration licence has a ten-year duration, and the production licence has a maximum duration of 50 years. US Internal Revenue Service, http://www. irs.gov/businesses/ article/0,,id=181552,00.html. In Nigeria the duration of an offshore oil prospecting licence is determined by the Minister and is between five and ten years. Deep Offshore and Inland Basin Production Sharing Contracts, Decree No 9 of 1999, as amended. Laws of the Federation of Nigeria, http://www.nigeria-law.org/DeepOffshoreAndInlandBasinProductionSharingContractsDecree1999. htm. It has been estimated that in the Gulf of Mexico a seven- to ten-year period is needed to bring a lease (licence to explore) to commercial production. Richard Ranger, senior policy consultant for the American Petroleum Institute, as cited in "Offshore drilling to take years to commence after expiration of ban," as cited in The Ledger.Com, http://www.theledger.com/article/20080925/news/809250388.

to the LOS Convention, prior to or during the life of a lease (see Box 1).[13] In comparison, Canada, which has considerable licensing activity on the Northwest Atlantic OCS, does not appear to have taken similar steps.

These events suggest that it is timely for OCS States and the Authority to commence consideration of their roles and responsibilities in the implementation of Article 82

---

[13] There have been several Notices of Sale for Outer Continental Shelf Leases accompanied by a Lease Stipulation concerning the Law of the Sea Convention Royalty, e.g. Oil and Gas Lease Sales: 178 Part 2 (Central Gulf of Mexico) in 2001; 180 (Western Gulf of Mexico, formerly Western Gap) in 2001; 190 (Central Gulf of Mexico) in 2003; 192 (Western Gulf of Mexico) in 2004. See MMS, http://www.mms.gov/. These Notices of Sale came in the wake of the recently delimited Mexico-US OCS boundary in the Gulf. More recently, Final Notice of Sale for Western Lease Sales 204 and 206, and for CPA Lease Sale 205 included the Law of the Sea Convention Royalty Payment stipulation. See Minerals Management Service, *Proposed Gulf of Mexico OCS Oil and Gas Lease Sale 207, Western Planning Area: Environmental Assessment*, OCS EIS/EA, MMS 2008-003, http://www. gomr.mms.gov/PDFs/2008/2008-003.pdf [hereafter Proposed GOM Lease 2008], at 6. In 2008, the Lease Stipulations, Oil and Gas Lease 207, Western Planning Area (Final Notice of Sale, 20 August 2008) re-state the Law of the Sea Convention Royalty Payment (Stipulation No. 4) and flesh out its application. See MMS, http://www.gomr.mms.gov/homepg/lsesale/207/fstips207.pdf [hereafter US Lease Stipulations]. The latest Stipulations apply to whole or partial blocks in the former Western Gap portion of the 1.4 nautical mile buffer zone north of the continental shelf boundary between the U.S. and Mexico, including blocks: Keathley Canyon portions of Blocks 978 through 980; Sigsbee whole Blocks 11, 57, 103, 148, 149, 194 and portions of Blocks 12-14, 58-60, 104-106, and 150. Proposed GOM Lease, ibid., at 6. For recent reporting on Gulf of Mexico leasing, see G. Ed Richardson et al., *Deepwater Gulf of Mexico 2008: America's Offshore Energy Future*, Minerals Management Service, OCS Report 2008-013.

Box 1: United States Lease Stipulations (Gulf Of Mexico, 2008)(Fn. 12)

WESTERN PLANNING AREA, OIL & GAS LEASE SALE 207 (20 AUGUST 2008) FINAL NOTICE OF SALE STIPULATION NO. 4 - LAW OF THE SEA CONVENTION ROYALTY PAYMENT

If the United States (U.S.) Government becomes a party to the 1982 Law of the Sea Convention (Convention) prior to or during the life of a lease issued by the U.S. Government on a block or portion of a block located beyond the U.S. Exclusive Economic Zone (EEZ) and subject to such conditions that the Senate may impose through its constitutional role of advice and consent, then the following royalty payment lease provisions will apply to the lease so issued, consistent with Article 82 of the Convention:

1. The Convention requires payments annually by coastal States party to the Convention with respect to all production at a site after the first 5 years of production at that site. Any such payments will be made by the U.S. Government and not the lessee.

2. For the purpose of this stipulation regarding payments by the lessee to the U.S. Government, a site is defined as an individual lease whether or not the lease is located in a unit.

3. For the purpose of this stipulation, the first production year begins on the first day of commercial production (excluding test production). Once a production year begins it shall run for a period of 365 days whether or not the lease produces continuously in commercial quantities. Subsequent production years shall begin on the anniversary date of first production.

4. If total lease production during the first 5 years following first production exceeds the total royalty suspension volume(s) provided in the lease terms, or through application and approval of relief from royalties, the following provisions of this stipulation will not apply. If, after the first 5 years of production but prior to termination of this lease, production exceeds the total royalty suspension volume(s) provided in the lease terms, or through application and approval of relief from royalties, the following provisions of this stipulation will no longer apply effective the day after the suspension volumes have been produced.

5. If, in any production year after the first 5 years of lease production, due to lease royalty suspension provisions or through application and approval of relief from royalties, no lease production royalty is due or payable by the lessee to the U.S. Government, then the lessee will be required to pay, as stipulated in paragraph 9 below, Convention-related royalty in the following amount so that the required Convention payments may be made by the U. S. Government as provided under the Convention:

    (a) In the sixth year of production, 1 percent of the value of the sixth year's lease production saved, removed, or sold from the leased area;

(b) After the sixth year of production, the Convention-related royalty payment rate shall increase by 1 percent for each subsequent year until the twelfth year and shall remain at 7 percent thereafter until lease termination.

6. If the U.S. Government becomes a party to the Convention after the fifth year of production from the lease, and a lessee is required, as provided herein, to pay Convention-related royalty, the amount of the royalty due will be based on the above payment schedule as determined from first production. For example, U.S. Government accession to the Convention in the tenth year of lease production would result in a Convention-related royalty payment of 5 percent of the value of the tenth year's lease production, saved, removed, or sold from the lease. The following year, a payment of 6 percent would be due, and so forth, as stated above, up to a maximum of 7 percent per year.

7. If, in any production year after the first 5 years of lease production, due to lease royalty suspension provisions or through application and approval of relief from royalties, lease production royalty is paid but is less than the payment provided for by the Convention, then the lessee will be required to pay to the U.S. Government the Convention-related royalty in the amount of the shortfall.

8. In determining the value of production from the lease if a payment of Convention-related royalty is to be made, the provisions of the lease and applicable regulations shall apply.

9. The Convention-related royalty payment(s) required under paragraphs 5 through 7 of this stipulation, if any, shall not be paid monthly but shall be due and payable to the Minerals management Service (MMS) on or before 30 days after the expiration of the relevant production lease year.

10. The lessee will receive royalty credit in the amount of the Convention-related royalty payment required under paragraphs 5 through 7 of this stipulation, which will apply to royalties due under the lease for which the Convention-related royalty accrued in subsequent periods as non-Convention related royalty payments become due.

11. Any lease production for which the lessee pays no royalty other than a Convention-related requirement, due to lease royalty suspension provisions or through application and approval of relief from royalties, will count against the lease's applicable royalty suspension or relief volume.

12. The lessee will not be allowed to apply or recoup any unused Convention-related credit(s) associated with a lease that has been relinquished or terminated.

3. RATIONALE AND BACKGROUND OF ARTICLE 82

3.1 Article 82

In the English text of the LOS Convention, Article 82 states that:

1. The coastal State shall make payments or contributions in kind in respect of the exploitation of the non-living resources of the continental shelf beyond 200 nautical miles from the baselines from which the breadth of the territorial sea is measured.

2. The payments and contributions shall be made annually with respect to all production at a site after the first five years of production at that site. For the sixth year, the rate of payment or contribution shall be 1 per cent of the value or volume of production at the site. The rate shall increase by 1 per cent for each subsequent year until the twelfth year and shall remain at 7 per cent thereafter. Production does not include resources used in connection with exploitation.

3. A developing State which is a net importer of a mineral resource produced from its continental shelf is exempt from making such payments or contributions in respect of that mineral resource.

4. The payments or contributions shall be made through the Authority, which shall distribute them to States Parties to this Convention, on the basis of equitable sharing criteria, taking into account the interests and needs of developing States, particularly the least developed and the land-locked amongst them.[14]

3.2 Prelude to the interpretation of Article 82

An analysis of Article 82 requires (1) the use of principles and rules of interpretation of the international law of treaties and (2) reference to the multilateral negotiations and treaty-making context of UNCLOS III and its rules of procedure.

3.2.1 Principles and rules of interpretation
in the international law of treaties

The principles and rules of the *Vienna Convention on the Law of Treaties*, 1969 (Vienna Convention) that assist the interpretation of Article 82 are set out in Part III (Observance, Application and Interpretation of Treaties) of that instrument.[15] These principles and rules are considered in two groups, namely (a) principles and rules concerning observance and application of a treaty and (b) principles and rules concerning the interpretation of treaties.

---

[14] LOS Convention, supra note 1, Art. 82.

[15] *Vienna Convention on the Law of Treaties*, Vienna, 23 May 1969, UN Doc. A/Conf.39/27; 1155 *U.N.T.S.* 331 (in force: 27 January 1980) [hereafter Vienna Convention].

(a) Observance and application of a treaty

Pact sunt servanda: once a treaty enters into force it becomes binding on States Parties to the treaty. States must perform their rights and obligations arising from the treaty in good faith.[16] This fundamental principle should be underscored because of the nature of the LOS Convention's "package deal" and the particular cross-provision compromise between Articles 76 and 82.

A State Party cannot justify non-performance of a treaty on the basis of its domestic law. For example, if Article 82 were to conflict with a domestic mineral royalty regime, that conflict will not excuse a State Party from performing its obligation under Article 82.[17]

Unless otherwise agreed, treaties are non-retroactive in application.[18] It is conceivable that a State may commence production on the OCS prior to its becoming a party to the LOS Convention. In this hypothetical scenario, Article 82 would begin to apply to that State only from the date of the entry into force of the treaty with respect to that State.

(b) Interpretation of a treaty

The Vienna Convention provides a general rule for the interpretation of treaties. The principle of good faith is at the basis of any treaty interpretation exercise and rules of construction are set out to give effect to this principle: an ordinary meaning is to be given to treaty terms; terms should be understood in their context; terms should be understood with reference to the object and purpose of the treaty.[19] While the general and ordinary meaning is sought, the purpose is to seek to understand the actual intention of the negotiators of the LOS Convention in the text they used.[20] The overall aim and purpose of the LOS Convention have to be borne in mind, implying that Article 82 has to be read within the Convention construed as a whole, rather than be construed in isolation.[21] Even so, giving meaning to a provision which appears in multiple and equally authentic texts may still be a difficult process.

Context for the purpose of interpretation is understood as including the treaty text (including preamble and annexes) and "any agreement relating to the treaty which was made between all the parties in connection with the conclusion of the treaty."[22] The preamble of the LOS Convention sets out the multiple objects and purposes of that instrument, frequently stated in a commitment towards the achievement of, *inter alia*, justice and equity, and in particular taking into account the special interests and needs of developing countries. This ethic, which was very much on the minds of UNCLOS III negotiators, underlies Article 82. The compromise reached consisted of the trade-

---

[16] Ibid., Art. 26.
[17] Ibid., Art. 27.
[18] Ibid., Art. 28.
[19] Ibid., Art. 31(1).
[20] McNair, supra note 5, 366.
[21] McNair, citing Harvard Research, Art. 19 and Hudson, ibid., 380-381.
[22] Vienna Convention, supra note 15, Art. 31(2)(a).

off between inter-linked Articles 76 and 82, enabling resolution of one of the last few hard-core issues standing in the way of adoption of the LOS Convention.

Also to be considered together with context in the interpretation of a treaty is any subsequent agreement or practice between States Parties which establishes their agreement concerning the interpretation or application of provisions.[23] Should the need to clarify the interpretation and application of Article 82 at a political, diplomatic or technical level arise, the Vienna Convention provides a legal basis for a possible "interpretation agreement" to facilitate implementation. There are useful precedents in relation to the LOS Convention, should an Article 82 interpretation or implementation agreement be deemed necessary.[24]

Should there continue to be doubt as to how Article 82 is to be interpreted, the Vienna Convention further provides that the *travaux preparatoires* and the circumstances of the conclusion of the LOS Convention may be used as supplementary means of interpretation to confirm the meaning of the provision arrived at by applying the general rule of interpretation.[25] Where the application of the general rule still leaves the meaning of a provision "ambiguous or obscure" or "leads to a result which is manifestly absurd or unreasonable", the *travaux preparatoires* may be used to determine the meaning of the provision.[26] It is conceivable that supplementary means of interpretation may be needed to arrive at a precise and reasonable interpretation of Article 82. The official records of UNCLOS III are essential for this exercise. Also invaluable for this purpose are the comprehensive collection of formal and informal documents of UNCLOS III, compiled by R. Platzöder,[27] and the multi-volume commentaries on the LOS Convention, sponsored by the Center for Oceans Law and Policy at the University of Virginia School of Law.[28]

---

[23] Ibid., Art. 31(3)(a).

[24] The Part XI Implementation Agreement was adopted by a resolution of the UN General Assembly and was the result of informal consultations among both States Parties and non-parties to the LOS Convention facilitated by the UN Secretary-General. The intention as set out in the Preamble is that "the Agreement shall be interpreted and applied together with Part XI as a single instrument" with the effect of modifying the interpretation of aspects of Part XI. *Agreement relating to the Implementation of Part XI of the United Nations Convention on the Law of the Sea of 10 December 1982*, in Compendium, supra note 1, 208–225 [hereafter Part XI Implementation Agreement]. A version consolidating the Agreement into the LOS Convention is available in Compendium, supra note 1. The implementation agreement concerning the LOS Convention's provisions on straddling fish stocks and highly migratory fish stocks has served to promote conservation and sustainable use objectives "through effective implementation of the relevant provisions of the Convention." *Agreement for the Implementation of the Provisions of the United Nations Convention on the Law of the Sea of 10 December 1982 relating to the Conservation and Management of Straddling Fish Stocks and Highly Migratory Fish Stocks*, New York, 4 December 1995, in Compendium, supra note 1, 271–305, Art. 2 at 272.

[25] Vienna Convention, supra note 15, Art. 32.

[26] Ibid.

[27] R. Platzöder, ed., *Third United Nations Conference on the Law of the Sea: Documents*, Vols. I–XVIII (Dobbs Ferry, N.Y.: Oceana Publications, 1982–1988).

[28] *United Nations Convention on the Law of the Sea 1982: A Commentary*, Vols. I-VI, Myron H. Nordquist, Series Editor-in-Chief (The Hague: Nijhoff, 1985-2002).

The LOS Convention authenticates the original treaty in six languages, namely Arabic, Chinese, English, French, Russian and Spanish.[29] The text of the LOS Convention is equally authentic in each of these languages. Under the Vienna Convention, the effect of this provision is that each text is equally authoritative in each language.[30] The LOS Convention makes no provision for one particular language text to prevail over all others. There is a presumption that the treaty provisions have the same meaning in each text.[31] However, it is conceivable that this might not be the case, despite the best efforts in drafting, possibly because of particular linguistic and/or juridical nuances in a language. In a hypothetical scenario where the general rule of interpretation and the supplementary means of interpretation do not remove differences in meaning between equally authentic texts, the Vienna Convention provides that "the meaning which best reconciles the texts, having regard to the object and purpose of the treaty, shall be adopted."[32]

3.2.2 Objects, context and process of UNCLOS III

The objects, context and process of UNCLOS III as a major multilateral law-making and codification conference will significantly inform the interpretation of its provisions. UNCLOS III was convened in 1973 as a result of a United Nations General Assembly Resolution to deal with "the establishment of an equitable international regime – including an international machinery – for the area and the resources of the sea-bed and ocean floor, and the subsoil thereof, beyond the limits of national jurisdiction, with a precise definition of that area and with a broad range of related issues including those concerning the regimes of the ... continental shelf ..."[33] The conference's future mandate to adopt a convention concerning all law of the sea matters was further clarified in a subsequent resolution.[34] That the Area and its resources were the common heritage of mankind and the benefits from the development of its resources would be shared equitably and, in particular, in the interests of developing countries was already a well-established premise for UNCLOS III. Two key, open issues relevant

---

[29] LOS Convention, supra note 1, Art. 320.

[30] Vienna Convention, supra note 15, Art. 33(1).

[31] Ibid., Art. 33(3).

[32] Ibid., Art. 33(4).

[33] UN General Assembly Resolution 2750 C (XXV), 17 December 1970, in Compendium, supra note 1, 365-367; Final Act of the Third United Nations Conference on the Law of the Sea, Montego Bay, 10 December 1982, Compendium, 306-339, para. 1 at 306; [hereafter Final Act]. Resolution 2750 was adopted together with Resolution 2749 (XXV) containing the Declaration of Principles Governing the Sea-Bed and the Ocean Floor, and the Subsoil Thereof, beyond the Limits of National Jurisdiction, Compendium, 360-363. These two resolution were preceded by a series of resolutions touching on the same themes in 1967 (2340, XXII), 1968 (2467, XXIII) and 1969 (2574, XXIV); Compendium, 349-360. A further string of resolutions following reports from the Seabed Committee were adopted in 1971 (2881, XXVI), 1972 (3029, XXVII) and 1973 (3067, XXVIII); Compendium, ibid, 363-375.

[34] UN General Assembly Resolution 3067 (XXVIII); Final Act, ibid., para. 6. The UN Secretary-General was earlier mandated by the General Assembly in Resolution 3029 A (XXVII) in 1972 to convene the first two sessions of UNCLOS III. Final Act, ibid., para. 5.

for the future Article 82 were the precise delimitation of the Area and the outer limit of the continental shelf; the two limits would, in effect, constitute the common boundary. Accordingly, the implicit linkage between Articles 76 and 82 was predetermined at a very early stage, and subsequently confirmed in the views of many delegations (see, for example, an informal suggestion by Seychelles, submitted in September 1978, in which it was stated in relation to draft articles 76 and 82 that "Seychelles considers that these two articles are indissociable and that they must be agreed to simultaneously" (NG6/3, 7 September 1978).

The UNCLOS III procedure is also a potentially significant aspect of the context for the interpretation of the LOS Convention. UNCLOS III adopted rules of procedure at the Second Session in 1974. The rules were accompanied by the important "Gentleman's Agreement", which was appended to the rules. The documents were approved by the General Assembly.[35] In particular, and in recognition of the close interrelation of issues to be negotiated at the conference and the need to produce a widely-acceptable convention, the Gentleman's Agreement stipulated that "[T]he Conference should make every effort to reach agreement on substantive matters by way of consensus and there should be no voting on such matters until all efforts at consensus have been exhausted."[36] The expectation at the beginning, and in subsequent practice, was that many issues in the LOS Convention would be negotiated in tandem. The state of negotiations would be reflected in the respective reports and successive drafts of the Chair of the Main Committee of the future convention, frequently indicating unsettled text and related proposals in square brackets. Because of the Gentleman's Agreement, the various negotiating texts would not be considered as being adopted until the entire text of the Draft Convention was put up for adoption. The requirement that there was to be no voting (except on occasional minor procedural matters) was meant to strengthen the consensus approach to collective decision-making, giving all delegations an equal voice. As it turned out, and despite preventative efforts, the Draft Convention was put up for voting. However, the main concern of those States that forced a vote was unrelated to Articles 76 and 82. For the purposes of analysis of Article 82 and its counterpart Article 76 provision, it is, thus, important to bear in mind the support for the inter-linkage of the two and the process that secured consensus on them.

3.3 Background and negotiating history of Article 82

The detailed diplomatic history of Article 82 has been recorded and commented upon in detail in the "Virginia Commentaries" and other literature.[37] Within the context of UNCLOS III, set out above, it is useful to briefly recount the origins of key ideas and

---

[35] Approved at the XXVIIIth session on 16 November 1973; Final Act, ibid., para 19.

[36] Final Act, ibid., para. 21.

[37] Satya N. Nandan and Shabtai Rosenne, vol. eds., *United Nations Convention on the Law of the Sea 1982: A Commentary*, Vol. 2 (Dordrecht: Nijhoff, 1993), commentary on Part VI, Article 82, at 930-947 [hereafter Nandan and Rosenne]; R. J. Dupuy and D. Vignes, eds., *A Handbook on the New Law of the Sea* (The Hague: Nijhoff, 1991), 375-381; A. Chircop and B. Marchand, "International Royalty and Continental Shelf Limits: Emerging Issues for the Canadian Offshore," 26(2) *Dal. L. J.* 273-302 (Fall 2003), at 283-293.

the milestones on the road to the diplomatic solution reached. The negotiation structure of UNCLOS III consisted of three main committees, each of which had several sub-committees and *ad hoc* groups working both on sessional and inter-sessional bases. Chaired by Andrés Aguilar (Venezuela) for most sessions and Reynaldo Galindo Pohl (El Salvador) for one session, the Second Committee was responsible for the negotiation of continental shelf issues. As noted earlier, UNCLOS III commenced with the premise set out in a General Assembly Resolution that the Area and its resources were the common heritage of mankind.[38] Although an early proposal, advanced by Malta, that national claims to the continental shelf should be frozen until the outer limits were defined was not pursued, the idea that coastal States should make contributions with respect to non-living resource development on the continental shelf caught on.[39] This was so because of the perception (correct as it turned out) that the more seaward the extent of the continental shelf, the more this would occur at the expense of the Area and common heritage of mankind.[40] The individual States' interest would be pursued at the expense of the international community interest.

Many coastal States approached continental shelf negotiations with the purpose of legitimizing greater claims to the seabed and its resources. Developing States were of the view that the continental shelf regime in customary law and as codified

---

[38] UN General Assembly Resolution 2749 (XXV), supra note 33. In his famous 1967 UN speech, Ambassador Arvid Pardo of Malta proposed that: "(1) The seabed and the ocean floor are a common heritage of mankind and should be used and exploited for peaceful purposes and for the exclusive benefit of mankind, as a whole. The needs of poor countries, representing that part of mankind which is most in need of assistance, should receive preferential consideration in the event of financial benefits being derived from the exploitation of the seabed and ocean floor for commercial purposes. (2) Claims to sovereignty over the seabed and ocean floor beyond present national jurisdiction, as presently claimed, should be frozen until a clear definition of the continental shelf is formulated." "Ocean Space," 1 November 1967, in Arvid Pardo, *The Common Heritage: Selected Papers on Oceans and World Order 1967-1974* (Malta: Malta University Press, 1975), at 41.

[39] Pardo also advocated that the coastal State should contribute to the international institutions a percentage of the revenue received from the exploitation of the living and non-living resources of a large zone of ocean space within its jurisdiction. Within what is now the EEZ, Pardo advocated a scale of contributions tied to the development of both living and non-living resources that the coastal State would make to international institutions. He envisaged four zones as follows: Area 1 -- 100 miles from the coast: no contribution; Area 2 – 100-150 miles: 25%; Area 3 -- 150-170 miles: 50%; Area 4 – 175-200M: 75%. Pardo, ibid., at 219–220. Writing in 1972, he optimistically guessed that around $200 million a year would be generated to the international institutions from hydrocarbon development alone. In "From Seabed Regime to Ocean Space Regime," 23 March 1972, in Pardo, ibid., 219-221. In 1971 Malta submitted the Draft Ocean Space Treaty as an attempt to envision what a new global law of the sea convention could look like, and within this instrument Article 61 provided: "1. The coastal State shall transfer to the International Ocean Space Institutions a portion of the revenue obtained from the exploitation of the natural resources of national ocean space. 2. The Institutions shall prepare a draft convention defining the contribution payable by coastal States to the International Ocean Space Institutions under paragraph one of this article and the modalities of payment." In "Draft Ocean Space Treaty," Working Paper submitted by Malta, A/AC.138/53, in Pardo, ibid, at 421.

[40] During the Second Session Switzerland stated that expanding the continental shelf to the edge of the continental margin so contracted the Area that it "was questionable whether an area truncated to that extent would even justify the establishment of an international authority to administer it." *Third United Nations Conference on the Law of the Sea: Official Records*, 2nd Session, Caracas, 20 June-29 August 1974 (New York: United Nations, 1975) [hereafter Second Session], at 157.

in the Geneva *Convention on the Continental Shelf*, 1958[41] served the interests of developed States, and UNCLOS III provided an opportunity to rectify this injustice.[42] Several land-locked and geographically disadvantaged States were not in favour of the extension of the continental shelf beyond 200 nautical miles as they perceived it to be an exclusive benefit for coastal States. When the objection could not be pursued further, they alternatively lobbied for equitable compensation or for rights of access to continental shelf mineral resources.[43] Other States recognized that coastal States were entitled to the full extent of the continental shelf, but that "they should share with the international community a portion of the natural resources of their continental shelves lying beyond 200 miles."[44] However, there were also yet other States that considered sharing as a form of encroachment on coastal State property rights.[45]

This divergence of views would lead the United States to propose, during the Second Session, that coastal State jurisdiction over the continental margin should be accompanied by a revenue-sharing scheme.[46] The foundations for the future Article 82 were laid in an informal working paper in August 1974.[47] A revised version of the working paper produced an alternative that did not yet focus exclusively on the OCS.[48]

---

[41] *Convention on the Continental Shelf*, Geneva, 29 April 1958, 499 *U.N.T.S.* 312-321.

[42] E.g., Singapore, Second Session, supra note 40, at 151.

[43] E.g., Uganda favoured compensation, Second Session, ibid., at 151. In response to ISNT Art. 63, Austria and the Group of Land-Locked and Geographically Disadvantaged States claimed participation rights (e.g., joint ventures, regional and sub-regional agreements) in the development of the continental shelf of regional coastal states. See Second Committee Informal Proposals, Platzöder, supra note 27, Vol. IV, at 323-327.

[44] E.g., Trinidad and Tobago, Official Records, Second Session, supra note 40, at 155.

[45] Burma (now Myanmar), Second Session, ibid., at 155.

[46] As reported in the report of the US delegation to the Second Session in Caracas, 20 June-29 August 1974, in Myron H. Nordquist and Choon-ho Park, eds., *Reports of the United States Delegation to the Third United Nations Conference on the Law of the Sea* (Honolulu: Law of the Sea Institute, 1983) [hereafter Nordquist and Park], at 69 and 72. The Dutch delegation also suggested adding a scale of contributions based on distance and depth.

[47] The paper contained a statement of principle that the coastal state should make contributions from the revenue derived from non-living resource development according to a scale. An international authority would distribute the contributions received. Second Committee, Informal Working Paper No. 3, 5 August 1974, Provision XII, in Platzöder, supra note 27, Vol. III, 288-295, at 292. Prepared by the Bureau, the paper contained ideas submitted in the Seabed Committee and UNCLOS III. At that point there was no agreement on the actual spatial application, although the early thinking contemplated areas within the 200M limit; Provision XII(2), ibid., at 292.

[48] This was Formula B: "The coastal State in the exercise of its rights with respect to the non-renewable natural resources of the continental shelf: (a) Shall comply with legal arrangements which it has entered into with other contracting States, their instrumentalities, or their nationals in respect to the exploration and exploitation of such resources; shall not take property of such States, instrumentalities or nationals except for a public purpose on a non-discriminatory basis and with adequate provision at the time of taking for prompt payment of just compensation in an effectively realizable form; and (b) Shall pay, in respect of the exploitation of such non-renewable resources seaward of the territorial sea or the 200-metre isobath, whichever is further seaward (insert formula), to be used, as specified in Article ..., for international community purposes, particularly for the benefit of developing countries." Informal Working Paper No. 3/Rev. 1, 12 August 1974, Provision XIII, in Platzöder, supra note 27, Vol. III at 301.

The paper referred to "revenue" rather than "volume" or "production" that would appear later. The Authority would distribute the revenue in the same way as revenue generated from the Area.[49]

It was not until the end of the Third Session in 1975 and the production of the Informal Single Negotiating Text (ISNT) that there emerged a common understanding on the basic principle that the coastal State would be obligated to make contributions related to the development of the OCS which would endure until the adoption of the LOS Convention (see Table 1, first column).[50] By this time the majority of delegations were in favour of the coastal State having at least 200M of EEZ and continental shelf. The remaining question concerned the criteria for determining the outer limit of the shelf (now understood as the outer edge of the continental margin) where this extended beyond 200M. However, the negotiation of the latter could not proceed without a compromise on revenue-sharing, and this was considered as the only way to achieve widespread support for the text.[51] Several positions were presented.[52] Major points of agreement in the ISNT text included the principle of a rising scale of payments which the Authority would be responsible for distributing to developing countries (see Table 1, first column).[53] There was also the idea of applying a grace period before the payment or contribution commenced to enable developers to recover the development costs.[54]

---

[49] The two alternative formulas that emerged in Provision VIII of Informal Working Paper No. 4/Rev. 2, 27 August 1974, were diametrically opposed. Formula A: "1. All States deriving revenues from the exploitation of the non-living resources of the ... zone shall make contributions to the international authority at the rate of ... per cent of the net revenues. 2. The international authority shall distribute these contributions on the same basis as the revenues derived from the exploitation of the international sea-bed area." Formula B: "The sovereign rights of the coastal State over its continental shelf are exclusive. The revenues derived from the exploitation of the continental shelf shall not be subject to any revenue sharing." Platzöder, supra note 27, Vol. III at 362.

[50] Informal Single Negotiating Text, ISNT/Part II, A/CONF.62/WP.8, 7 May 1975, in Platzöder, supra note 27, Vol. I at 31.

[51] US delegation report on the Third Session, Geneva, 17 March-9 May 1975, in Nordquist and Park, supra note 46, at 98-99.

[52] The Group of Land-Locked and Geographically Disadvantaged States initially advocated rights of participation in the exploration and exploitation of continental shelf resources. Eventually, they proposed that the coastal State make payments or contributions in kind. Proposals of the Group and Austria concerning Article 69 (ISNT II), dated 11 April 1976, Platzöder, supra note 27, Vol. IV at 325-327. However, both proposals included payments and contributions related to the development on shelf areas at a depth of 200 metres or 50 miles from the coast. Austria proposed a 5% rate for the area within 200M, and 10% for the area beyond. Ibid., at 325-326. The US proposed that the coastal State be left with the discretion regarding the form of the payment or contribution. The procedure would be agreed upon by State Parties. Ibid., at 326.

[53] There continued to be disagreement on whether an exemption from contributions in favour of developing OCS States should be included. Ibid.

[54] The US was disposed to agree to revenue-sharing relating to activities beyond 200M (in contrast to earlier disposition to areas beyond the territorial sea or the 200-metre isobath). It considered the need for an initial grace period of five years (i.e., a period to enable some initial cost-recovery and during which the revenue-sharing would not apply), after which the contribution would be at the rate of one per cent for the sixth year, increasing thereafter by one per cent per year until the tenth year when it would reach five per cent. The latter figure would remain the ceiling for subsequent production. The more economically productive phase was understood to occur after the first five years of production. The applicable value to determine the contribution was thought to be the well-head value. Ibid.

Another proposal was profit-sharing (i.e., payment on the net revenue), but this was not considered practical because of the perceived unpredictability of deep-sea drilling costs and the "great difficulty in reaching agreement among States of differing economic systems on what costs can be deducted from gross profits to compute net revenues."[55] OCS producers were expected to recover a substantial portion of their development costs during the grace period during which no royalty would be payable.

By the time the Revised Single Negotiating Text (RSNT) was produced to reflect the state of consensus at the Fifth Session in 1976, there was widespread support for the application of payments and contributions to the OCS (see Table 1, second column).[56] There was support for a grace period, a rising scale for payments or contributions and that the amount would be based on value or volume of production. There remained to be agreed the length of the grace period and the payment ceiling. Lack of agreement on this last point continued until the production of the first version of the Informal Composite Negotiating Text (ICNT) during the Sixth Session in 1977 (see Table 1, third column).[57] Eventually, the issue of the rate of contribution was resolved through a private negotiating group chaired by Frank Njenga (Kenya). The United States continued to insist upon a maximum rate of 5 per cent whereupon the representative of Singapore made a counter-proposal of 12 per cent, which was immediately rejected by the United States. In order to seek a compromise on this issue, the representative of Austria proposed 7 per cent as a maximum rate, which was acceptable to all members of the group except the United States, which reserved its position. This figure was later inserted into the negotiating text when it was accepted without further comment by any delegation. (Helmut Tuerk, Chairman of the Austrian Delegation, UNCLOS III, presently Judge of the International Tribunal for the Law of the Sea, pers. comm.) There were also differences on which developing countries would be exempted from the obligation and whether the Authority should receive the payments.[58] The remaining differences were resolved in the first revision of the ICNT and the full text of Article 82 as it is in the LOS Convention appeared (Table 1, fourth column).[59]

---

[55] Ibid.

[56] Revised Single Negotiating Text, Part II, A/CONF.62/WP.8/Rev. 1/Part II, 6 May 1976, in Platzöder, supra note 27, Vol. I, at 218. Even the latest proposal of Austria in response to the RSNT, Article 70, supported the OCS as basis for payments and contributions. Platzöder, ibid., Vol. IV at 471.

[57] Informal Composite Negotiating Text, A/CONF.62/WP.10, 15 July 1977, in Platzöder, ibid., Vol. I at 318.

[58] The following Paragraph 4 to RSNT Article 70 was submitted by the US: "The payments or contributions referred to in paragraphs 1 and 2, shall be made to an appropriate entity of the United Nations. The Parties to this Convention shall agree on necessary payment and other relevant procedures. The entity shall distribute these payments to States Parties to this Convention on the basis of equitable sharing criteria, taking into account the interests and needs of developing countries, especially the land-locked and geographically disadvantaged among them, as well as developing countries which have made payments or contributions in accordance with paragraph 1 and 2 of this article." Platzöder, ibid., Vol. IV at 471.

[59] The maximum rate of seven percent was reached at this time. Informal Composite Negotiating Text/ Revision One, ICNT/Rev. 1, A/CONF.62/WP.10/Rev. 1, 28 April 1979, in Platzöder, ibid., Vol. I, at 423. The subsequent negotiating texts were: Informal Composite Negotiating Text/Revision Two, ICNT/Rev. 2, A/CONF.62/WP.10/Rev. 2, 11 April 1980, in Platzöder, ibid., Vol. II, 3-175, at 51.; Draft

The negotiation history of Article 82 would not be complete without reference to a particular contribution of the land-locked and geographically disadvantaged States. In 1979 these States proposed the establishment of a Common Heritage Fund (CHF).[60] The CHF proposal was aimed primarily at the EEZ, but also mentioned Article 82, and was motivated by concerns that the size of the Area was being reduced. This view produced two proposals. First, in return for the encroachment on the Area, they felt that payments and contributions should be made also with reference to the EEZ.[61] Second, they proposed that payments and contributions pursuant to Article 82 be made into the Common Heritage Fund through the Authority for distribution as benefits to developing countries on an equitable basis.[62] However, this late proposal did not gain consensus and no further major change to Article 82 occurred.[63] As will be seen below, the idea of a Common Heritage Fund could be a useful procedural mechanism for the contemporary implementation of Article 82.

Convention on the Law of the Sea (Informal Text), A/CONF.62/WP.10/Rev. 3, 22 September 1980, in Platzöder, ibid., 227; Draft Convention on the Law of the Sea, A/CONF.62/L.78, 28 August 1981, ibid., 409–410.

[60] Introduced on 17 August 1979 and fully explained in a background paper at the 1980 New York Session. The original idea appears to have been first advanced by Nepal in 1978. See also Letter to all Heads of delegations by the Organizing Committee of the Group for the Common Heritage Fund (signed by Austria and Nepal), 12 February 1980, in Platzöder, supra note 27, Vol. IV, 531. The other group members included Afghanistan, Bolivia, Lesotho, Singapore, Uganda, Upper Volta and Zambia. See also "Background Paper on the Common Heritage Fund Proposal," New York Session 1980, in Platzöder, ibid., Vol. IV, 528–530 [hereafter Background Paper].

[61] "In our view the case for the CHF is very strong. In many forums the world community has declared that it intends to establish a New International Economic Order, based on a redistribution of global resources. However, very little has been done to move us toward that goal. We think that the Common Heritage Fund is a logical – if rather modest – first step toward the New International Economic Order," Background Paper, ibid., at 529.

[62] Background Paper, ibid., 528.

[63] Only minor changes were made, e.g., replacing "developing country" by "developing state." See Nandan and Rosenne, supra note 37, 945.

TABLE 1: EVOLUTION OF ARTICLE 82 IN UNCLOS III

- ISNT, 1975, Art. 69	- RSNT, 1976, Art. 70	- ICNT, 1977, Art. 82	Art. 82 of : - ICNT Rev. 1, 1977 - ICNT Rev. 2, 1980 - Draft Convention (Informal Text), 1980 - Draft Convention, 1981 - LOS Convention, 1982
1. The coastal State shall make payments or contributions in kind in respect of the exploitation of the non-living resources of the continental shelf beyond 200 nautical miles from the baselines from which the breadth of the territorial sea is measured.	1. The coastal State shall make payments or contributions in kind in respect of the exploitation of the non-living resources of the continental shelf beyond 200 nautical miles from the baselines from which the breadth of the territorial sea is measured.	1. The coastal State shall make payments or contributions in kind in respect of the exploitation of the non-living resources of the continental shelf beyond 200 nautical miles from the baselines from which the breadth of the territorial sea is measured.	1. The coastal State shall make payments or contributions in kind in respect of the exploitation of the non-living resources of the continental shelf beyond 200 nautical miles from the baselines from which the breadth of the territorial sea is measured.
2. The rate of payment or contribution shall be ... per cent of the value or volume of production at the site. Production does not include resources used in connection with exploitation.	2. The payments and contributions shall be made annually with respect to all production at a site after the first five years of production at that site. For the sixth year, the rate of payment or contribution shall be ... per cent of the value or volume of production at the site. The rate shall increase by ... per cent for each subsequent year until the tenth year and shall remain at ... per cent thereafter. Production does not include resources used in connection with exploitation.	2. The payments and contributions shall be made annually with respect to all production at a site after the first five years of production at that site. For the sixth year, the rate of payment or contribution shall be one per cent of the value or volume of production at the site. The rate shall increase by one per cent for each subsequent year until the tenth year and shall remain at five per cent thereafter. Production does not include resources used in connection with exploitation.	2. The payments and contributions shall be made annually with respect to all production at a site after the first five years of production at that site. For the sixth year, the rate of payment or contribution shall be one per cent of the value or volume of production at the site. The rate shall increase by one per cent for each subsequent year until the twelfth year and shall remain at seven per cent thereafter. Production does not include resources used in connection with exploitation.

TABLE 1: EVOLUTION OF ARTICLE 82 IN UNCLOS III (CONTD.)

3. The International Authority shall determine the extent to which developing countries shall be obliged to make payments or contributions provided for in paragraphs 1 and 2.	3. The International Authority shall determine if and to what extent developing countries shall be obliged to make payments or contributions provided for in paragraphs 1 and 2.	3. A developing country which is a net importer of a mineral resource produced from its continental shelf is exempt from making such payments or contributions in respect of that mineral resource.	3. A developing country/State* which is a net importer of a mineral resource produced from its continental shelf is exempt from making such payments or contributions in respect of that mineral resource.
4. The payments or contributions provided for in paragraphs 1 and 2 shall be made to the International Authority on terms and procedures to be agreed upon with the Authority in each case. The International Authority shall distribute these payments and contributions on the basis of equitable sharing criteria, taking into account the interests and needs of developing countries.	4. The payments or contributions shall be made to the International Authority on terms and procedures to be agreed upon with the Authority in each case. The International Authority shall distribute these payments and contributions on the basis of equitable sharing criteria, taking into account the interests and needs of developing countries, particularly the least developed amongst them.	4. The payments or contributions shall be made through the Authority, which shall distribute them to States Parties to the present Convention, on the basis of equitable sharing criteria, taking into account the interests and needs of developing countries, particularly the least developed and the land-locked amongst them.	4. The payments or contributions shall be made through the Authority, which shall distribute them to States Parties to this Convention, on the basis of equitable sharing criteria, taking into account the interests and needs of developing countries/ States*, particularly the least developed and the land-locked amongst them.

With ICNT Rev.2, the precise wording that would appear in the LOS Convention was adopted. The last change was substitution of 'state(s)' for 'country(ies)' in paragraphs 3 and 4.

Source: Adapted from A. Chircop and B. Marchand, "International Royalty and Continental Shelf Limits: Emerging Issues for the Canadian Offshore," 26(2) Dalhousie Law Journal 273–302 (Fall 2003).

4. RELATIONSHIP OF ARTICLE 82 TO OTHER PROVISIONS IN THE LOS CONVENTION

In general, it is obvious that all provisions of the LOS Convention bear a relationship to each other because collectively they form the package deal of this instrument. However, there are specific provisions of the Convention that have a more direct relationship to Article 82 and should be profiled to assist the more in-depth analysis reserved for later in the report. Other relevant provisions are considered later in the report where appropriate.

4.1 Relationship with Article 76

As indicated, Article 82 has a particular *quid pro quo* relationship with Article 76. Collectively, the two provisions reflect the negotiators' intentions, and since adoption of the Convention, also the intentions of States Parties that the benefit which the coastal State enjoys from the exploitation of non-living resources of the OCS is accompanied by the collateral or contingent obligation in Article 82.

Although a coastal State's entitlement to the continental shelf is *ipso iure* and *ab initio*, the definition of the outer limit of the continental shelf is subject to scientific and technical criteria set out by the LOS Convention and which the coastal State needs to satisfy. The coastal State must satisfy the appurtenance test before it can proceed with the definition of the outer limit of the OCS, otherwise it would encroach on what is legitimately the seabed and subsoil of the Area. The procedure for the definition of the outer limit is set out in the Convention and includes consideration by the Commission on the Limits of the Continental Shelf (CLCS), an expert international body established in that instrument for this purpose.[64] On completion of this procedure, including taking into consideration the recommendations of the CLCS, if any, the coastal State can proceed to establish the outer limits of its continental shelf, which shall then be final and binding.[65] At the time of writing, several States Parties made Article 76 submissions to the CLCS.[66]

---

[64] The CLCS is established under Annex II of the LOS Convention, supra note 1. The CLCS has prepared several documents to guide OCS States in the preparation of their submissions. See Division for Ocean Affairs and the Law of the Sea, http://www.un.org/Depts/los/clcs_new/clcs_home.htm [hereafter DOALOS].

[65] LOS Convention, supra note 1, Art. 76(8).

[66] As at 1 June 2009 the following States had made submissions: 2001 – Russian Federation; 2004 – Brazil; Australia; 2005 – Ireland (Porcupine Abyssal Plain); 2006 – New Zealand; Joint Submission by France, Ireland, Spain and United Kingdom (Celtic Sea and Bay of Biscay); Norway; 2007 – France (French Guiana and New Caledonia); Mexico (western portion of Gulf of Mexico); 2008 – Barbados; United Kingdom (Ascension Island); Indonesia (north west of Sumatra); Japan; Joint Submission by Mauritius and Seychelles (Mascarene Plateau); Suriname; Myanmar; 2009 – France (French Antilles and Kerguelen Islands); Yemen (south east of Socotra); United Kingdom (Hatton Rockall); Ireland (Hatton Rockall); Uruguay; Philippines (Benham Rise); Cook Islands (Manihiki Plateau); Fiji; Argentina; Ghana; Iceland (Ægir Basin and western and southern Reykjanes Ridge); Denmark (north of the Faroes); Pakistan; Norway (Bouvetøya and Dronning Maud Land); South Africa (mainland of the territory of the Republic of South Africa); Joint submission by the Federated States of Micronesia,

In addition to identifying the full spatial extent of the coastal State's sovereign rights over the continental shelf, Article 76 serves the purpose of defining the potential area that is captured by the coastal State's obligation in Article 82. It is conceivable that exploitation of non-living resources occurs before the outer limit of the continental shelf is established in accordance with the Convention's procedure. There is nothing in the LOS Convention which suggests that Article 82 would not apply to a State Party in relation to the exploitation of OCS resources before the outer limit is actually established. The application of Article 82 is not contingent on the actual definition of the outer limit of the OCS.

4.2 Relationship with Part XI

The Area and its resources are vested in mankind as a whole and are not subject to national appropriation.[67] The Authority was specifically established to act on behalf of mankind in the Area.[68] Activities in the Area are to be carried out for the benefit of mankind and taking into consideration the interests and needs of developing States and peoples who have not yet attained independence or are self-governing.[69] "The Authority shall provide for the equitable sharing of financial and other economic benefits derived from activities in the Area through any appropriate mechanism, on a non-discriminatory basis ..."[70] The provisions on benefits accruing from mineral resource development in the Area, although not identical, share similar developmental purposes as Article 82 payments and contributions.

A recent report of the Committee of the International Law Association is of the view that "Article 82 ... provides for the application of the Common Heritage Principle within the OCS, even though the OCS is within the coastal State's maritime jurisdiction."[71] In brief, the justification put forward for this view is that the Article 82 obligation was the *quid pro quo* for broad margin States to be able to define the OCS beyond the 200M limit. The outer limits of national jurisdiction, or for that matter the limits of the Area, were not defined at the outset of Article 82 negotiations. Clearly, the negotiating history of Article 82 is evidence of this trade-off, but not necessarily for the proposition that the trade-off was intended as an application of the common heritage principle. The difficult

---

Papua New Guinea and Solomon Islands (Ontong Java Plateau); Joint submission by Malaysia and Viet Nam (southern part of the South China Sea); Joint submission by France and South Africa (Crozet Archipelago and the Prince Edward Islands); Kenya; Mauritius (Rodrigues Island); Viet Nam (North Area, VNM-N); Nigeria; Seychelles (Northern Plateau Region); France (La Réunion Island and Saint-Paul and Amsterdam Islands); Palau; Côte d'Ivoire; Sri Lanka; Portugal; United Kingdom (Falkland Islands, and of South Georgia and the South Sandwich Islands); Tonga; Spain (Galicia); India; Trinidad and Tobago; Namibia and Cuba.

[67] LOS Convention, supra note 1, Arts. 136 and 137(1).

[68] Ibid., Arts. 137(2), 156 and 157. All States Parties to UNCLOS are *ipso facto* members of the Authority. Because the Authority acts on behalf of and for the benefit of mankind, it presumably acts, or should act, also in the interests of non-States Parties.

[69] Ibid., Art. 140(1).

[70] Ibid., Art. 140(2).

[71] International Law Association, Committee on the Outer Continental Shelf, "Report on Article 82 of the UN Convention on the Law of the Sea (UNCLOS)," Rio De Janeiro Conference, 2008, http://www.ila-hq.org/en/committees/index.cfm/cid/33 [hereafter ILA Report], at 2, para. 1.3.

UNCLOS III negotiation process does not evidence the final consensual intention of the negotiators (as distinct from the numerous negotiating exchanges) to characterize the obligation to make payments or contributions as an application of the common heritage principle. On the contrary, the finalized text expressly limits the application of the common heritage principle to Part XI, i.e., to the Area and its resources, and Article 82 eschews altogether any reference to the principle.[72] Further, the rule that payments and contributions have to be made through the Authority is not necessarily additional evidence of the application of the common heritage principle;[73] the Authority has other tasks allocated to it by the Convention that do not necessarily or directly relate to its primary mandate of organizing and controlling activities in the Area.[74] Accordingly, in the view of this report, although Article 82 payments and contributions are for the benefit of States Parties to the Convention, they are not an application of the common heritage principle. This is because the OCS and its resources are subject to the coastal State's sovereign rights and are separate from the common heritage principle. In all probability, the value of this discourse is essentially a scholarly one and does not bear on the interpretation and implementation of the provision.

Pardo's original idea, on the eve of UNCLOS III, was for the payment to be made to the International Ocean Space Institutions that would emerge from the conference. UNCLOS III negotiators initially had different views on an appropriate international organization in Article 82. There were proposals designating the Authority as a beneficiary of the payments or contributions, but they did not receive the support necessary and were thus not included in the negotiating texts.[75] The eventual compromise was to give the Authority the role,[76] but limited it to receiving payments and contributions for the purpose of distribution to States Parties.

For present purposes, it is clear that it is only the provisions in Part XI that provide the basis for the Authority's mandate to implement Article 82. There are roles for both the Assembly and Council. The Assembly is the supreme organ of the Authority and is empowered "to establish general policies in conformity with the relevant provisions of this Convention on any question or matter within the competence of the Authority."[77] The Council is the Authority's executive organ and has the power to establish specific policies on any matter within the Authority's competence, but within the more general policies of the Assembly.[78] These are discussed in more detail below (6.3.1).

---

[72] As noted in the earlier discussion of the negotiating history of Article 82, a proposal to establish a Common Heritage Fund in part out of the Article 82 payments and contributions did not find sufficient support at UNCLOS III. This could possibly be further indication of the intention of UNCLOS III negotiators to detach the Article 82 obligation from the common heritage principle.

[73] During the negotiation of Article 82, it was not always beyond doubt that the Authority would be the institution tasked with passing on the payments and contributions to States Parties. The reference to "International Authority" in the ISNT and RSNT was still a generic reference at the time.

[74] For example, Article 275-276 concerning the establishment of national marine scientific research and technological research centres provide an interesting additional role for the Authority. LOS Convention, supra note 1.

[75] Nandan and Rosenne, supra note 37. See especially the discussion at the Sixth Session at 940 et seq.

[76] The US had proposed that the payments and contributions could be directed at a UN body or regional economic organization. Nandan and Rosenne, ibid., 941.

[77] LOS Convention, supra note 1, Art. 160(1).

[78] Ibid., Art. 162(1).

Specifically for Article 82 purposes, the Council has been assigned the power to:

> ... recommend to the Assembly rules, regulations and procedures on the equitable sharing of financial and other economic benefits derived from activities in the Area and the payments and contributions made pursuant to Article 82, taking into particular consideration the interests and needs of developing States and peoples who have not attained full independence or other self-governing status ...[79]

The Assembly will consider the Council's recommendations. It may approve them or "return them to the Council for reconsideration in the light of the views expressed by the Assembly."[80] The roles of the Council and Assembly will be analyzed later in the report.

4.3 Other LOS Convention provisions

As indicated earlier, States have a duty under general international law and the international law of treaties to perform in good faith a treaty to which they are parties (*pacta sunt servanda*).[81] This basic duty is reiterated in the LOS Convention and the Convention further imports the doctrine of abuse of rights. Thus, States Parties have an obligation to "fulfill in good faith the obligations assumed under this Convention and shall exercise the rights, jurisdiction and freedoms recognized in this Convention in a manner which would not constitute an abuse of right."[82] This provision is of particular significance for OCS States which, as will be seen later in the report, have a responsibility to implement the obligation within their municipal system. Although they have a choice as to *modus* of implementation, they must do so within the letter and spirit of Article 82 and the Convention as a whole. The Authority is also likely in a position to invoke this provision *vis-à-vis* OCS States.

Although it is unlikely that any State party to the LOS Convention would contemplate denunciation of the Convention, there is a provision in this regard which has some relevance for Article 82. Denunciation is the act by which a State formally withdraws from a treaty. Article 317 provides for the procedure for denunciation of the Convention which takes effect one year after notice is communicated to the United Nations Secretary-General. Of particular interest here is the provision that a State "shall not be discharged by reason of the denunciation from the financial and contractual obligations which accrued while it was a Party to this Convention ..."[83] The effect is that the Article 82 obligation to make payments or contributions would persist after a State ceases to be a party. The denunciation provision further stipulates that the denunciation shall not "affect any right, obligation or legal situation of that State created through the execution of this Convention prior to its termination for that State."[84] A State that defines the outer limit of the OCS in accordance with Article 76 would continue to enjoy sovereign rights over the OCS, even after denouncing the Convention.

---

[79] Ibid., Art. 162(2)(o)(i).
[80] Ibid., Art. 160(2)(f)(i).
[81] Vienna Convention, supra note 15, Art. 26.
[82] LOS Convention, supra note 1, Art. 300.
[83] Ibid., Art. 317(2).
[84] Ibid.

5. CONTENT OF ARTICLE 82

5.1 Nature of the obligation

Classifying the legal obligation in Article 82 poses a challenge because the provision is unprecedented. Generic text is used to describe the obligation in Article 82. The obligation is stated as a payment or contribution, with no obvious hint of how UNCLOS III intended to characterize the obligation.

Resort to an equivalent concept from the fiscal frameworks for oil and gas and other mining industries helps to better classify the obligation, precisely because it is these kinds of activities whose production will be captured by the provision. In the oil and gas industry, payments that are due as compensation for the use of property calculated as a percentage of receipts on the basis of an account per unit produced are called royalties. In effect, the royalty payment constitutes a share of the profit to the property owner.[85] In relation to offshore activities, the "property owner" is frequently the State, so that the payment of royalty is due to the crown as a condition in the production licence.[86] With the caveat that the payments and contributions in Article 82 do not conform to normal characteristics of a royalty within the domestic setting (e.g., the Authority or for that matter beneficiary States are not "property owners" of OCS non-living resources), it is convenient to characterize the obligation as a type of international royalty. One scenario for its implementation in a domestic setting, and to the extent (if at all) that a State party would pass on the financial burden to producers, would likely be in the form of a royalty payment to the licensing authorities. The royalty collected would then be the basis for the OCS State to make the payments and contributions contemplated in Article 82.

The obligation is not called a "tax," which, if it were, could well have constituted the first international tax. Elsewhere, it has been stated that the concept of "tax" is tied to the sovereign's right to levy monies in support of government and public programmes and services, and to enforce the payment of such monies pursuant to legislative authority.[87] The power to make tax assessments necessarily accompanies the power to enforce payments. The LOS Convention does not provide the Authority with this power. The idea of classifying payments and contributions in relation to production from activities within national jurisdiction as tax probably would have been too novel

---

[85] *Black's Law Dictionary*, 8th ed. (St. Paul, MN: Thomson/West, 2005). The MMS defines royalty as follows: "A share of the minerals produced from a lease; a percentage of production either in money or in kind that a Federal Lease is required to pay." Outer Continental Shelf: Oil and Gas Leasing Procedures Guidelines, OCS Report MMS 2001-076, New Orleans, October 2001, p. 85, http://www.gomr.mms.gov/PDFs/2001/2001-076.pdf.

[86] Elsewhere, Chircop has noted that another similarity to the domestic royalty is the element of compensation for Area loss to the OCS state as a result of Article 76. A major difference is that the payment and in-kind contribution are due not to the licensing state, and not even to the ISA, but to States Parties. Aldo Chircop, "Operationalizing Article 82 of the United Nations Convention on the Law of the Sea: A New Role for the International Seabed Authority?" 18 *Ocean Yb* 395-412 (2004), at 400.

[87] Chircop, ibid., 398-399.

and unprecedented at the time.[88] Indeed, the Authority is not the recipient beneficiary of the payments and contributions; OCS States make payments or contributions *through* the Authority.

Article 82 does not address the question of compensation to the Authority for performing its responsibilities in regard to Article 82. Nor has the Authority been expressly enabled to recover the bare costs for providing the services it is expected to render. The general operating expenses incurred by the Authority are covered elsewhere in the Convention.[89] When the LOS Convention empowers the Authority to recover particular administrative costs, it does so expressly as in the case of a fee for processing an application for approval of a plan of work in the Area.[90] However, as will be discussed below, there is a good argument for an implied power for the Authority to recover the fair and reasonable expenses it incurs in discharging its Article 82 responsibilities.

5.2 Key elements of the obligation

Apart from a few specific provisions concerning the functions of the Council and Assembly, the LOS Convention provides little guidance to States Parties and the Authority on how Article 82 might be implemented. In order to consider potential options for the implementation, it is helpful to deconstruct the article in order to understand its component parts and how collectively those parts aim to achieve the purposes of the provision. The anatomy of Article 82 is set out in the template in Table 2. It is derived from the express text alone. Article 82 has a basic rule and a number of collateral rules that set out the framework for the implementation of the provision. The analysis follows the template in Table 2.

---

[88] "Taxation of activities undertaken as sovereign rights is in itself a *sovereign* power of the state, and thus it is unlikely that negotiating states would have agreed to the creation of a taxation function in a global international organization. Even in relation to activities in the Area, there is no utilization of domestic law fiscal concepts connoting the exercise of sovereign functions, and instead reference is made to 'payment,' a generic concept connoting a financial obligation and no more." Chircop, ibid., at 399.

[89] LOS Convention, supra note 1, Art. 173.

[90] Examples of this in the LOS Convention are Art. 162(2)(p) and Annex III, Art. 13(2) and (3). Ibid.

TABLE 2: TEMPLATE OF ARTICLE 82

Nature of rule	Rule	Elements
Basic rule	The OCS State shall make payments or contributions in kind in respect of the exploitation of non-living resources of the OCS.	OCS State has a choice between making (1) payments or (2) contributions in kind.
		Payments and contributions relate to non-living resources.
		Payments and contributions relate to exploitation leading to production.
Collateral rules concerning payments or contributions in kind.	Payments or contributions shall be made annually.	Payments or contributions shall be made regularly on an annual basis.
	Payments or contributions shall be made with respect to all production.	Payments and contributions are to be based on all production.
		Payments and contributions shall be calculated on the value or volume of production.
		Production does not include resources used in connection with exploitation.
	Payments or contributions commence on the sixth year of production and are based on a pre-set scale.	Grace period: obligation to make payments or contributions does not apply to the first five years of production.
		Pre-set scale: payments and contributions commence on the sixth year of production, on a scale starting at 1% of production in the sixth year and increasing by 1% per year until it reaches 7% in the twelfth year, which thereafter shall remain the ceiling.

TABLE 2: TEMPLATE OF ARTICLE 82 (CONTD.)

Nature of rule	Rule	Elements
Collateral rule concerning eligibility to make payments and contributions.	Net importing OCS developing States are exempted from making payments or contributions.	Exemption for OCS developing States: if a developing OCS State imports more of the resource subject to payments or contributions than it exports, it is exempted from the obligation in relation to that resource.
Collateral rule concerning distribution of benefits.	Payments and contributions are to be made through the Authority, which shall distribute them to States Parties.	Payments or contributions are to be made through the Authority.
		Beneficiary States: the Authority will distribute payments and contributions to States Parties on the basis of equitable sharing criteria, taking into account the interests and needs of developing States, especially the least developed and land-locked States.

5.2.1 The OCS State shall make payments or contributions in kind in respect of the exploitation of non-living resources of the OCS

(a) Choice between making (1) payments or (2) contributions in kind

Article 82 provides the OCS State with the choice of discharging its obligation either by making payments *or* making contributions in kind. The timing of the decision on the manner of discharge rests with the OCS State.

The text of Article 82 suggests that the obligation could be discharged in various ways. The choice of language stipulating how the obligation may be discharged is interesting. In the English language, payment means the act of passing on remuneration (monies or equivalent) to discharge an obligation.[91] UNCLOS III negotiators shied away from "payments in cash or in kind." Instead, they chose to refer to payments and in-kind contributions, suggesting they intended to distinguish between monetary discharges and in-kind discharges of the obligation. "Contributions" does not necessarily connote a lesser sense of obligation than payments, because in the English language (including in

---

[91] *Oxford English Dictionary*, Comp. Ed. (Oxford: Oxford University Press, 1971; 26th US Printing) [hereafter OED].

legal English), and although it may connote an element of voluntariness, a contribution may be levied as one's part to a common fund, loss or liability.[92] "Contributions in kind" offers a more flexible interpretation than "payments." The OCS State may elect to discharge its obligation in a non-monetary form, but of equivalent value. For example, it may elect to discharge the obligation by transferring a share of the volume of the produced natural resource, such as crude oil, natural gas or minerals.

The text used to capture "payments or contributions in kind" in the other authentic texts of the LOS Convention leads to additional observations.[93] The Spanish text is a virtual mirror reflection of the English text: *pagos o contribuciones en especie*. Although a sister Romance language to Spanish, the French text is *contributions en espèces ou en nature*. Rather than *paiements* (or *payements*), which would be closer to payments and *pagos*, the drafters of the French text preferred to use the concept of *contribution* for both payments and contributions in kind. In French *contribution* can also be used for payment.[94] After the first paragraph setting out the basic obligation, the French text proceeds to use "contribution" in the rest of Article 82 as an abbreviated reference to both payments and contributions in kind. Despite the different approach to drafting of the French text, the general meaning conveyed appears to be the same as the English and Spanish texts.[95] There is a more nuanced difference relating to "contributions in kind" in the Chinese text: 实物 (*shi wu*, in Mandarin). The concept of "in kind" in Chinese connotes a material element (e.g., goods or produce) thus excluding any notion of an abstract in-kind contribution.[96]

Article 82 does not allocate the responsibility for the determination of the precise quantity of the payment or contribution (described as a percentage of value or volume) that may be due. One conceivable reading of this provision is that this is an implicit responsibility of the OCS State, with a potential practical role for the licenced producer in the OCS State to play. There is nothing in the text of Article 82 that suggests a role for the Authority in this regard, such as an "assessment" power. Clearly, the OCS State will be better informed than the Authority on eligible volumes of production, as these will tend to fluctuate with reference to market conditions, technical matters and the size and life of a field. Values can be determined only if the volumes are known. However, because the Authority is mandated with the responsibility to receive the payments or contributions, it is reasonable to suggest that at a minimum the Authority should be informed of the basis for the determination of value or volume and the amounts that are due in the opinion of the OCS State.[97]

---

[92] OED, ibid.

[93] Curiously, the title of Article 82 in English, French and Spanish is also inconsistent. The English and Spanish texts use an abbreviated reference to contributions (rather than to "contributions in kind"). This is not the case with the French text.

[94] *Le petit Robert*, (Paris: Dictionnaires Le Robert, 2002); Raymond Guillen and Jean Vincent, *Lexique de termes juridiques* (Paris: Dalloz, 1988).

[95] Personal communication from Gwénaëlle Le Gurun, Legal Officer, Office for Legal Affairs, International Seabed Authority, Kingston, Jamaica, November 2008.

[96] *The Pinyin Chinese-English Dictionary* (Beijing: Foreign Languages Institute, 1985); *A Modern Chinese-English Dictionary* (Beijing: Foreign Language Teaching and Research Press, 2001). Also, personal communication from Kening Zhang, Senior Legal Officer, Office for Legal Affairs, International Seabed Authority, Kingston, Jamaica, November 2008.

[97] On the role of the Authority in this regard, see Michael W. Lodge, "The International Seabed Authority:

The provision does not stipulate that the choice is subject to a one-time decision by the OCS State that will be the basis for all future discharges of the obligation; nor does it expressly stipulate that the option is open on an annual basis. The question arises as to whether an OCS State that opts for payment of monies in year six, when the obligation starts to apply, can change this to a contribution in kind in year seven? Does the exercise of the first option foreclose all future options? The same question potentially applies to whether the OCS State has to continue to use value or volume as the basis for the determination of the payment or contribution after the exercise of the first option. The question can be approached from perspectives of legal interpretation and implementation convenience. A plain legal reading of the text of Article 82 does not preclude change of discharge options. From the perspective of implementation convenience, it is conceivable that the OCS State (and the Authority for that matter) will find it simpler to discharge its obligation using the same expressed option and accompanying procedure. But it is conceivable that over a 20-year life span of a petroleum field (for example) the OCS State may wish to change the manner of discharging the obligation.

While the obligation must be discharged by the OCS State, presumably the OCS State may internally allocate the responsibility to effect the payments or contributions due to a domestic or domestically-licenced entity, although at international law the OCS State remains responsible for the discharge of the obligation. Its decision will be influenced by whatever option it chooses to discharge the obligation and on whether it decides to internally absorb the cost at the national level or pass it on to other entities. It may simply delegate the discharge to a governmental institution, with payments to be made from consolidated national revenues. If the resource concerned is exploited by a national mining or oil company (crown corporations or parastatal bodies), or possibly even by a licenced private producer, the OCS State may, conceivably, direct (by regulation or contract) that entity to make the payments or contributions in kind. In the case of the United States Lease Stipulations, the MMS will receive the royalty payments after the expiration of a production lease year so that the U.S. Government will make the required Article 82 payments.[98]

Another somewhat comparable example is the contributions levied from entities in States Parties and paid to the International Oil Pollution Compensation Fund (IOPCF).[99]

Its Future Directions," in Myron H. Nordquist, John Norton Moore and Tomas H. Heidar, eds., *Legal and Scientific Aspects of Continental Shelf Limits* (Leiden: Brill, 2004), 403-409.

[98] US Lease Stipulations, supra note 13, para. 9. The text of the Lease Stipulation 4 suggests that the US is anticipating it will make payments, rather than contributions in kind: "Any such payments will be made by the U.S. Government and not the lessee." Ibid., para. 1, repeated in para. 5.

[99] The original instrument is *International Convention on the Establishment of an International Fund for Compensation for Oil Pollution Damage*, London, 18 December 1971, 1110 *U.N.T.S.* 57, establishing the 1971 Fund. The 1971 Fund terminated in 2002. The current 1992 Fund was established the *Protocol to Amend the International Convention on the Establishment of an International Fund for Compensation for Oil Pollution Damage, 1971*, London, 27 November 1992, 1996 A.T.S. 3 (in force on 30 May 1996). Amendments in 2000 raised the compensation amounts. In 2003 a Supplementary Fund was established by the *Protocol of 2003 to the International Convention on the Establishment of an International Fund for Compensation for Oil Pollution Damage, 1992*, London, 16 May 2003, IMO Doc. LEG/CONF.14/20 (in force on 3 March 2005). For up-to-date versions of the amended Convention and rules and procedures of the 1992 Fund and Supplementary Fund, see International Oil Pollution Compensation Funds, http://www.iopcfund.org/.

The 1992 Fund consists of monies paid by entities in member states that receive more than 150,000 tonnes of "contributing oil" (crude or heavy fuel oil) transported by sea. States Parties to IOPCF inform the Fund of the quantities of oil received and in turn the Fund invoices those entities directly.[100]

If the OCS State opts to make the payments, there could be a practical issue concerning the currency of the monies of the payment, a matter which the LOS Convention does not address. In the interests of convenience and minimization of potential fluctuation in the value of the payments, the Authority should expect payment in a convertible currency, although this is not expressly required by the Convention.[101] This is a reasonable inference because the Authority would be distributing payments and contributions to designated beneficiaries. For the sake of clarity, the currency for discharging the obligation should be addressed in an agreement between the OCS State concerned and the Authority.

If the OCS State decides on making contributions in kind, i.e., in the form of a percentage of the volume of the produced resource, there could be a different practical matter for the Authority to deal with, namely the need to make arrangements for the receipt of the resource, transportation needs and risk management arrangements (e.g., insurance). There would be costs associated with "receiving," "holding," and "distributing" the contributions, responsibility for the costs of which are not addressed in Article 82. This will not be without precedent at the domestic level. In the United States the Minerals Revenue Management of the MMS has a Royalty-in-Kind programme (RIK) which provides the federal government with the option of receiving production royalty payments in value or in kind.[102] Although the RIK is sold in the market, there is a prequalification requirement for traders. A major difference in this case is that the RIK is for the benefit of the federal government, thus giving it flexibility in its disposition, whereas the Authority cannot benefit from in-kind contributions.

(b) Payments and contributions related to non-living resources

The Article 82 obligation concerns production from the exploitation of *non-living resources*. It will be recalled that the OCS State exercises sovereign rights over the continental shelf in relation to its natural resources, which are defined as "mineral and other non-living resources of the sea-bed and subsoil together with living organisms belonging to sedentary species …"[103] The sedentary species of the OCS could be

---

[100] Not all States Parties proceed on this basis. For example, the Canadian contribution to the IOPCF is not paid by domestic entities, but by the Ship-Source Oil Pollution Fund established under the *Marine Liability Act*. See Chircop and Marchand, supra note 37, at 295.

[101] In relation to the Enterprise (which is not yet operational) the issue of currency was left open. For example, it was anticipated that the Enterprise might need to make a public sale of its obligations in financial markets or the currency of a State Party, and if the currency of a State Party was to be used, to obtain the approval of that State Party. LOS Convention, supra note 1, Annex IV, Art. 11(2)(a). The ILA report is of the view that the payment *must* be in the form of an internationally tradable currency or a related type of convertible payment such as Special Drawing Rights because Article 82(4) stipulates that the payment will be distributed to developing countries. ILA Report, supra note 71, para. 2.10.

[102] MMS, MRM Royalty-in-Kind Program, http://www.mrm.mms.gov/RIKweb/RIKStratRead.htm.

[103] LOS Convention, supra note 1, Art. 77(1) (2) and (4).

economically valuable, for example lobster, crab and scallops. As seen above, early proposals for what would become Article 82 attempted to include living resources in the EEZ, but this demand was resisted by broad margin states.[104] Thus, Article 82 is limited to non-living resources; a case of *inclusio unius exclusio alterius*. The concept of non-living resources still includes a wide range of resources. Minerals are naturally occurring inorganic substances, often additionally characterized by particular crystal and chemical structures, which when mined can be valuable commodities. Other non-living resources include hydrocarbons (namely petroleum, natural gas and gas hydrates) which, in contrast to minerals, are organic compounds.

5.2.2 Payments and contributions shall be made annually

Article 82 foresees the making of payments or contributions in kind on an annual basis. There are two points to be made here. The first concerns the meaning of "annually," which is intended to refer to periodicity, and which may be taken to mean the calendar year or financial year, which might not coincide, and both of which might vary from country to country. The second point is that it is likely that the value of the payment or volume of the contribution might vary from year to year in response to market and other conditions. The wide fluctuation of prices of hydrocarbons and other mineral commodities, as well as hard currency values in recent times suggests there could be a potential issue in the implementation of Article 82. The timing of payments or contributions could potentially and significantly affect the value of the payment or contribution. It would be important for the OCS State and the Authority to agree on a regular schedule of payments and contributions, rather than leaving these to be made at any time within a 12-month period. In the case of the United States, the Lease Stipulations for the OCS in the Gulf of Mexico specify that a production year runs for 365 days a year commencing from the date of commencement of production (excluding test production), and irrespective of whether there is continuity in commercial production.[105] Thus a nine-month production period in a given calendar year still constitutes annual production.

5.2.3 Payments and contributions shall be made with respect to all production

(a) Payments and contributions are to be based on all production

An important question concerning the calculation of the OCS Royalty is whether the payments and contributions in kind are to be calculated on the basis of the gross

---

[104] Early proposals in anticipation of and during UNCLOS III included all resources of the EEZ, but by the time the first negotiating text was produced it was clear that the duty would have a limited resource and spatial application. Coastal States became increasingly reluctant to share resources or related benefits that were otherwise subject to the exclusive sovereign rights of exploration and exploitation. Insofar as the EEZ was concerned (and continental shelf up to 200M), the idea of sharing was whittled down to the surplus of fisheries (but not sedentary species) in that zone. Informal Single Negotiating Text (ISNT), 1975, Art. 69, in Platzöder, supra note 27, Vol. I, 31. LOS Convention, supra note 1, Arts. 62, 69-72.

[105] US Lease Stipulations, supra note 13, para. 3.

or net of commercial production.[106] Commercial production clearly excludes test production. The reference in Article 82 to "all production" as the basis for the making of annual payments and contributions appears to suggest the gross rather than the net production as the basis for the calculation.[107] Although costs are significantly lower at the production stage, this provision does not permit deduction of costs incurred before the value or volume is determined for payment or contribution purposes. During the negotiation of Article 82, a Working Paper proposed to apply the royalty on the net. This proposal did not receive sufficient support and negotiators opted for what appeared to be the simpler solution.[108] It was anticipated that it would be difficult to agree on what cost elements need to be deducted to determine the net revenue.[109]

Another consideration at this point is the OCS State's discretion in determining how much production should take place. It would exercise this discretion with reference to market conditions for the commodity concerned. The effect for the consequent payments and contributions is that these will fluctuate with the level of authorized production.

(b) Payments and contributions shall be calculated on the value or volume of production

Closely related to the question concerning "all production" is the phrase "value or volume of production." This is a term that requires clarification with reference to the moment in time used to determine value or volume, and whether the application of one or the other would produce the same result. It is not entirely clear what is meant by "value" of production at the site. In the case of hydrocarbons, one interpretation is that it refers to the "well-head value" referring to the time when the resource is captured and brought to the surface.[110] For other minerals, it may be less clear. The implication is that the market price per barrel (in the case of petroleum) is the fair market value at the well-head at a given moment in time. It is reasonable to assume that UNCLOS III negotiators must have intended that value or volume would have equal or comparable worth, so that there would not be a substantial difference between discharging the obligation by the making of payments, as compared to contributions in kind.

(c) Production does not include resources used in connection with exploitation

The calculation of production for the purpose of determining the amounts of payments and contributions will be based on product that is ready for market

---

[106] Chircop and Marchand, supra note 37, 297-298.

[107] Chircop and Marchand, ibid. The ILA Report comes to a similar conclusion on this point. supra, note 71, para. 2.8.

[108] Provision VIII, Informal Working Paper No. 4/Rev. 2, 27 August 1974, Formula A: "1. All States deriving revenues from the exploitation of the non-living resources of the ... zone shall make contributions to the international authority at the rate of ... per cent of the net revenues. 2. The international authority shall distribute these contributions on the same basis as the revenues derived from the exploitation of the international sea-bed area." Platzöder, supra note 27, Vol. III, 362. This was the US position. Nordquist and Park, supra note 46, 98-100.

[109] US delegation report on the Third Session, Nordquist and Park, ibid.

[110] US delegation report on the Third Session, Geneva, 17 March-9 May, 1975 in Nordquist and Park, supra note 46, at 98-99.

distribution or processing. Production does not include resources used in connection with exploitation. In the case of hydrocarbons, for example, this means that any gas used for re-injection into the reservoir to enhance production or which may be flared, would be excluded from the calculation.[111]

5.2.4 Payments and contributions shall be based on a pre-set scale

(a) The grace period

Article 82 foresees a grace period of five years during which no OCS royalty is due and within which the producer is expected to recoup the development costs. Over the next seven years the OCS royalty will increase progressively. Until the maximum rate is reached, it is arguable that the producer will continue to be able to recoup earlier costs, while at the same time production costs should diminish progressively. By the time the full rate of seven per cent is applicable, the more profitable period in the commercial life of the field will have commenced. This formula was probably based more on the need for a compromise than on the realities of cost-recovery. There were alternative proposals at the negotiating table, but none achieved sufficient support.[112]

It is conceivable that the grace period may cause difficulties for producers. Given the expensive modern day offshore development in a deep water environment, it remains to be seen whether the grace period and the progressively incremental rate are sufficient for a developer to recoup development costs as was intended by the UNCLOS III negotiators. An illustration of the potential problem here is with reference to current deep-water drilling in the Gulf of Mexico, which has been provided with incentives such as deep water royalty relief to encourage investment in a high cost and high risk environment.[113] The producer is permitted to produce the resource before any royalty obligations are due. The matter of cost-recovery is a complex one and will depend on a number of variables including the field concerned, the difficulty of the geology, market value of the product and regulatory obligations. The ability to recover costs may vary over the life of the field depending on commodity prices. The United States Lease Stipulations had to address the particular issue of coordinating royalty relief with the Article 82 OCS royalty in the event it accedes to the LOS Convention.[114]

---

[111] Chircop and Marchand, supra note 37, at 296.

[112] Early proposals would have levied different percentages on the production depending on whether it occurred within or outside 200M. An Austrian proposal proposed contributions of up to five or ten percent. See Chircop and Marchand, supra note 37, at 289.

[113] *Deep Water Royalty Relief Act*, 30 CFR Part 203, introduced by President Clinton as part of Public Law 104–58 to provide incentives for the development of new supplies of energy. The royalty incentives were intended to promote investment in the deep waters of the Gulf of Mexico, which were considered to carry particularly high costs and risks. The region was considered to be particularly promising and has in fact become one of the most important domestic sources for oil and gas. Federal Register (Rules and Regulations), Vol. 73 (No. 195), 7 October 2008, at 58468. See also Energy Information Administration, http://www.eia.doe.gov/oil_gas/natural_gas/analysis_publications/ngmajorleg/continental.html.

[114] US Lease Stipulations, supra note 13, paras. 4, 5 & 7.

One way of looking at this potential issue is that it is the responsibility of the OCS State to meet this obligation and how it does so should not be of concern to other LOS Convention States Parties and the Authority. The OCS State may decide to implement Article 82 in its domestic royalty regime, effectively passing on the cost to producers. In this scenario it is up to the OCS State to establish or adjust its domestic royalty regime to accommodate the Article 82 obligation. The OCS State may decide to provide domestic royalty relief to spur OCS development and production. The OCS State decides what cost (consisting of domestic royalty relief and meeting the Article 82 obligation) it is willing to incur in order to proceed with offshore development and eventual production.

The grace period is also, arguably, a period that would allow the OCS State to accumulate domestic royalty income before being obliged to make payments and contributions thereafter. In the offshore licensing practices for oil and gas (for example) of some coastal States, the initial years of production may be characterized by lower domestic royalties to assist with the recovery of field exploration and development costs. Thereafter, royalties would be expected to increase. For Article 82 purposes, unless the government of an OCS State absorbs the fiscal responsibility for payments or contributions, it is likely that the producer can expect a mixture of applicable royalties and royalty rates.

(b) Pre-set scale

Table 3 sets out the scale of payments and contributions in kind. Payments and contributions commence on the sixth year of production, on a scale starting at one per cent of production in the sixth year and increasing by one per cent per year for the next four years until it reaches the maximum rate of seven per cent in the twelfth year, which thereafter shall remain the annual rate thereafter

TABLE 3: SCALE OF PAYMENTS AND CONTRIBUTIONS

Production year	Scale in terms of % of value or volume
Years 1 to 5	0
Year 6	1
Year 7	2
Year 8	3
Year 9	4
Year 10	5
Year 11	6
Year 12 and subsequent years	7

The grace period provides relief for the recovery of the exploration and development costs, but there is no further relief for costs incurred thereafter. As noted earlier, the assessment system set out in Article 82(2) is based on "all production from a site," and therefore would not enable the recovery of the production and eventual decommissioning costs once the site reaches the end of its commercial life.

5.2.5 Exemption for OCS developing States

Article 82 provides an exemption from the application of the obligation of making payments or contributions with respect to the *exploitation of non-living resources* to OCS developing States which are *net importers of the mineral resource* produced on their OCS.[115] Other developing OCS States that are not net importers of the mineral resource concerned would be required to make payments or contributions. The purpose of this provision is to bestow a benefit on particular developing OCS States. The benefit is not a general exemption from making payments or contributions, but only from making such payments or contributions in relation to a mineral resource of which it is a net importer.

There is a drafting problem which concerns whether the reference to "mineral resource" in Article 82(3) is intended to provide for a narrower application of the exemption in that provision to a category of non-living resources, i.e., only mineral resources. This provision is consistently drafted in the English, French and Spanish texts. If the general obligation applies to non-living resources, should the exemption intended to provide a benefit to developing OCS States not also apply to all non-living resource exploitation?

As seen earlier, in Article 77(4) the LOS Convention appears to implicitly differentiate between mineral resources and other non-living natural resources. Article 77 is an important provision that sets out the rights of coastal States over the continental shelf. Article 82 conditions the exercise of those rights on the OCS by subjecting them to an obligation. It is not apparent why Article 82(3) refers only to mineral resources (inorganic matter), which could technically be read as excluding hydrocarbons (organic matter). The Vienna Convention provides that treaty terms, although to be given their ordinary meaning, should be read in their context and in the light of the object and purpose of the treaty. An interpretation of Article 82(3) requires a reading within the context of Article 82 and the broader context of Part VI on the continental shelf. It is submitted that Article 82(3) (a collateral rule) should be read consistently with the basic rule set out in 82(1). Resort to supplementary means of interpretation, namely the *travaux preparatoires*, does not remove the inconsistency as the negotiating history does not fully explain the reason for the difference. However, to the extent that the negotiating history does not indicate any intention of negotiators to distinguish between mineral and other non-living resources for Article 82 purposes, it reinforces the reading that the collateral exemption rule should be read consistently with the basic rule.

---

[115] During negotiations of this provision there were differences on whether the exemption should apply to all OCS States. The ensuing compromise was limited to developing States as per Article 82(3). See Nandan and Rosenne, supra note 37, 946–947.

5.2.6 Payments and contributions are made through the Authority for distribution to beneficiaries

(a) Payments and contributions are to be made through the Authority

OCS States make payments or contributions *through*, not to, the Authority. This means the payments and contributions are not made to benefit the Authority. However, in a practical sense, the contributions and payments will need to be made in the first instance to the Authority in order for the distribution process envisaged by this provision to work.

After the OCS State opts to make payments or contributions, there is no indication as to the determination of actual amounts, currency(ies) to be used for payments, delivery of contributions in kind, timing of payments or contributions, and so on. Much will depend on the goodwill of the OCS State which has a continuing good faith obligation.[116]

The Authority will need to be informed of the amount and/or form of the payments and contributions as it will need to make the necessary administrative arrangements to perform its distributive role. It is conceivable that the Authority could undertake basic desk top monitoring of eligible activities on continental shelves around the world, but this would be short of auditing activity because it does not have a mandate to do so. In any case, such auditing would be practically impossible. The OCS State does not have an express duty to inform the Authority on any OCS matter, with the possible exception of the actual payments or contributions that are due.[117] It might not be possible to compel an OCS State to disclose the information needed for the Authority to perform its role.[118]

To ensure smooth transfers of payments and contributions, it will be advisable for the Council to recommend a framework to the Assembly for the administrative responsibilities of Article 82, but which can accommodate *ad hoc* arrangements between the Authority and individual OCS States. Such arrangements should address how the obligation will be performed by the OCS State concerned (payment or contribution), the value or volume calculated and the basis of the calculation, modalities of payments or contributions, timing of payments and contributions, and so on.

A potentially serious issue for the Authority is that Article 82 does not make provision for the Authority to cover its own administrative costs. The article provides only for the unqualified distribution of payments or contributions to States Parties. While

---

[116] LOS Convention, supra note 1, Art. 300.

[117] In certain circumstances, it may be possible for the coastal State to argue that there is no duty under the Convention, even with reference to the fulfillment of a conventional obligation, to disclose information which might be contrary to the essential interests of its security. LOS Convention, ibid., Art. 302. There is an argument that the ISA may have to monitor activities on the extended shelf in the case of a joint development zone that includes, with its consent, the adjacent International Seabed Area.

[118] There are precedents for this. For example, several States have not provided the IOPCF the information required for the Fund to determine "contributing oil" to assess the amount of contributions to the Fund from eligible entities in those States. *International Oil Pollution Compensation Funds: Annual Report 2002* (London: IOPCF, 2002), 27. Every year, the annual Funds report list States that do not provide reports. See the latest *International Oil Pollution Compensation Funds: Annual Report 2007* (London: IOPCF, 2007), http://www.iopcfund.org/AR07_E.pdf, at 25 and 164.

on the one hand the Authority's funds are based on a variety of sources listed in Article 171, which include (until such time as seabed mining takes place on a commercial basis) assessed contributions of all States Parties to the administrative budget of the organization, it appears to be unreasonable to expect the Authority to incur costs for the administration of Article 82 responsibilities without being able to even recover its overhead costs. This would be at odds with the current practice of international organizations tasked with the administration of trust funds and donor funding. The United Nations practice in establishing and administering trust funds is to charge a 15 per cent overhead charge.[119] It would not be unreasonable to enable the Authority to charge overhead consistent with this practice, which would also reduce the amount to be paid by States Parties in the form of assessed contributions to the administrative budget.

The question of costs has another dimension to it insofar as contributions in kind are concerned. If the OCS State opts to make contributions in kind, the Authority would likely incur additional costs relating to the receiving, storage and transportation of such contributions, among other costs. There could be customs and export procedures to manage. The ideal scenario for the Authority is to make arrangements with the OCS State (possibly including the licenced producer) to liquidate the contribution in kind by putting it on the market. This could be covered by the Article 82 Agreement and the costs incurred by the OCS State could then be deducted or charged against the proceeds. This would be a reasonable and practical arrangement which would assist in achieving the general purposes of Article 82. For this to happen it will be necessary to interpret Article 82 to accommodate such costs.

One way of harmonizing the apparent conflict between text that does not appear to permit deductions for costs and the reality that costs will be incurred is to distinguish between (1) the calculation of the royalty amounts, from (2) the process of taking delivery of and administering the royalty received. The bare text of Article 82 is clear insofar as the calculation of the royalty amount is concerned, i.e., that there can be no deductions by the OCS State. As to the process of taking delivery of and administering the amounts received, the fair costs incurred by the Authority in this regard and the assistance provided by the OCS State in liquidating contributions, insofar as they are consistent with existing practices in such situations, could be interpreted as being reasonably included and necessary for the implementation of Article 82 in a contemporary context. In other words, "fair costs" ought to be deductible from the royalties received. However, for the sake of clarity, it would be important for the Authority to seek the endorsement of its membership for this interpretation.

(b) Beneficiaries

Article 82(4) stipulates that the Authority is to distribute payments and contributions to the designated beneficiaries on the basis of equitable sharing criteria. The Authority is already provided with initial guidance on the distribution of benefits, but will need more detailed criteria to effectively address the requirements of this provision.

---

[119] United Nations Development Programme. The World Bank charges a 15% administrative fee for donor funds.

In principle, Article 82(4) provides for all States Parties to the LOS Convention to benefit from Article 82 payments and contributions. Payments and contributions will be distributed by the Authority on the basis of equitable sharing criteria, which, ostensibly, will need to be developed by the Authority. The Authority will need to develop more detailed criteria within the framework of Article 82(4), and in particular:

(1) taking into account the interests and needs of developing States; and
(2) giving particular consideration to the interests and needs of least developed and land-locked developing States;

and Article 162(2)(o)(i):

(3) "taking into particular consideration the interests and needs of developing States and peoples who have not attained full independence or other self-governing status."

There are two noticeable inconsistencies between Article 82(4) and Article 162(2)(o)(i). First, peoples who have not attained independence or self-governing status are not mentioned in Article 82(4) (see (3) above). Article 82(4) seems to focus on States Parties, whereas such peoples will clearly not have yet attained statehood, let alone become parties to the LOS Convention. Second, and unlike Article 82(4), Article 162(2)(o)(i) does not include particular consideration of the specific interests and needs of the least developed (among developing States) and land-locked developing States (see (2) above). For the purposes of Article 82(4) it is suggested that the inconsistency should not be read as substantive because the two provisions provide criteria that are cumulatively applicable to the distribution of benefits in Article 82. This could be more of an issue for the Council's responsibility in developing equitable criteria for the distribution of benefits from activities in the Area, because Article 82(4) is unrelated to activities in the Area. There is an argument to be made for the equitable criteria yet to be developed for Article 82(4) and the equitable criteria for the distribution of benefits from the Area to be synonymous, despite the inconsistent drafting.

The text concerning distribution of payments and contributions suffers from ambiguity. Presumably "taking into account" implies preferential consideration. What is intended by "interests and needs," and according to whom, is not clear. For example, are developing States with basic livelihood needs on a par with developing States that wish to reduce their dependence on imported energy?[120] Hence the need for the Authority to conceptualize a hierarchy of needs that will inform the equitable criteria it is expected to apply. In theory, it is conceivable to foresee a tentative general ranking as follows:

(1) least developed land-locked States Parties and peoples who have not attained full independence or other self-governing status;
(2) other developing States Parties (including other land-locked developing states); and

---

[120] Chircop, supra note 86, at 409.

(3) other States Parties (including newly industrialized, developed land-locked, developed states generally).[121]

The Authority would need to consider what States should be considered least developed and developing, presumably by reference to authoritative international indices.[122] It is reasonable to expect that this list will change over time. Also, the negotiating history of UNCLOS III and the LOS Convention's requirement to consider equitable criteria suggest that the situation of developed land-locked States and geographically disadvantaged States may also have to be considered.

An interesting question arises as to whether the developing OCS State claiming the Article 82(3) exemption from making payments or contributions, may benefit from the payments and contributions of other OCS States. There is nothing in the provision which suggests that such a State may not be able to benefit. Whether such a State may benefit *pari passu* with other developing States, or to any other extent, will depend on the equitable sharing criteria developed by the Authority. After all, the developing OCS State claiming the exemption continues to enjoy OCS rights (the *quid pro quo* of Article 82), which could be an equitable criterion giving it lower ranking.

Developing equitable criteria to distribute benefits will be a complex exercise. During the 1970s, the political distinctions between North and South, and East and West were more obvious than they are today. The distinction between developed and developing States was primarily with reference to GDP per capita, then the dominant development index. In the contemporary context the differentiation between States in various stages of economic and social development needs more solid justification than a simple monetary measure of welfare. There is greater emphasis on human well-being within the State. The differentiation required by Article 82 that would be relevant in a contemporary context might need to consider a range of indices and indicators, not necessarily restricted to national summaries for States, such as the Human Development Index (HDI) maintained by UNDP and the World Development Indicators (WDI) developed by the World Bank. Article 82 benefits should also reach peoples who are not yet independent or self-governing. The World Bank has classified its member States and other economies with populations in excess of 30,000 inhabitants according to geographic region, income group and lending category.[123] Geographic regions include low-income and middle-income economies, which are generally understood as developing economies.[124] The income group is divided according to 2007 GNI per capita.[125] The

---

[121] Ibid., 409-410.

[122] Other equitable criteria might include socio-economic status and mineral resource dependence. For example, newly industrialized States might not have as much a need to receive payments and contributions as much as other developing States.

[123] World Bank, http://web.worldbank.org/WBSITE/EXTERNAL/DATASTATISTICS/0,,contentMD K:20420458~menuPK:64133156~pagePK:64133150~piPK:64133175~theSitePK:239419,00.html.

[124] There is an important clarification attached to this: "The use of the term is convenient; it is not intended to imply that all economies in the group are experiencing similar development or that other economies have reached a preferred or final stage of development. Classification by income does not necessarily reflect development status." World Bank, ibid.

[125] This is done by using the World Bank Atlas method. The income groups are set out as follows: low

lending category consists of States with a low per capita income that affects their financial ability to borrow monies from the World Bank.[126]

There will be advantages and disadvantages associated with the use of any particular index. For example, the highly respected and independently-produced HDI aims at "putting people at the centre of development" in the process of defining "developing countries." It has the advantage of identifying human inequities, reveals inequalities which may be buried in national statistics and constitutes a useful tool for policy-making. At the same time, some may appear (at least intuitively) to be of concern for Article 82 purposes.[127] The criteria used for the HDI do not measure environmental concerns.[128] The World Bank categories, although updated regularly, are useful from a monetary perspective but do not necessarily give a full picture of developmental status.[129] There are other potentially useful indices and indicators, such as the Human Poverty Index (HPI) and the World Bank's Poverty and Natural Resource Indicators that may be useful in adding other developmental dimensions.[130]

Taking these factors into account, the Authority might want to consider a range of indices to develop its own composite index of rankings and reflecting equitable criteria.[131] A composite index of its own, while convenient and tailored to Article 82 purposes, will not be without disadvantages.[132] Among other, if poorly constructed or improperly interpreted, it could give a misleading message, inviting simplistic policy conclusions and political challenges from member States of the Authority. The index would need to be constructed in a transparent manner and using sound statistical and conceptual principles.

A major issue with Article 82(4) is the ultimate purpose and application of the payments and contributions in kind passed on to the beneficiaries. There is no indication

---

income, $935 or less; lower middle income, $936 - $3,705; upper middle income, $3,706 - $11,455; and high income, $11,456 or more. World Bank, ibid.

[126] In 2007 this figure was less than $1,095. World Bank, ibid.

[127] For example Cuba is listed in the "high" category with other and mostly developed States, while Haiti is ranked as "medium" and well above the "low" category.

[128] E.g., literacy and life expectancy. The HDI measures three capabilities: length of a health life and life expectancy at birth; knowledge, as measured by adult literacy rates and gross enrolment at primary, secondary and tertiary education levels; and standard of living, measured by GDP per capita in purchasing power parity (PPP). UNDP, *Measuring Human Development: A Primer* (New York: UNDP, 2007), http://hdr.undp.org/en/media/Primer_complete.pdf [hereafter HDI Primer], 36.

[129] For example, China is classified as high income, despite the uneven level of development in non-urban areas.

[130] HDI Primer, supra note 128, 67.

[131] A composite index has been defined as follows: "In general, a composite index is a unit-less number that combines various indicators or statistics to convey a larger picture. A composite index is formed when individual indicators are compiled into a single index on the basis of some underlying model. Ideally, a composite index should measure a multidimensional concept that cannot be captured by a single indicator alone—such as poverty, competitiveness, sustainability, market integration, etc." HDI Primer, ibid., 20.

[132] Disadvantages of composite indices are discussed by M. Nardo et al., *Handbook on Constructing Composite Indicators: Methodology and User Guide,* OECD Statistics Working Paper (Paris: OECD, 2005).

that these funds should be destined for any particular purpose or to achieve any objective. Even if one were to assume that insofar as developing countries are concerned, the benefits are intended to address developmental needs, the application of the benefits remains vague. Indeed, it will be difficult to develop equitable sharing criteria with reference to interests and needs without a sense of the application of the payments and contributions. Earlier in the discussion of the negotiation history of this provision, reference was made to a proposal for a Common Heritage Fund. This idea has been revived recently and could serve an administrative function as a "holding fund" for the eventual distribution of payments and contributions.[133]

While equitable criteria should relate to interests and needs within the objects, purposes and framework of the LOS Convention, in a contemporary context this necessitates reference to current major processes such as the Millennium Development Goals (MDGs), climate change adaptation and integrated coastal and ocean management (ICOM). Adopted at the United Nations Millennium Summit in 2000, the MDGs set various developmental targets that include, *inter alia*, poverty eradication, protection of the common environment, protecting the vulnerable and meeting the special needs of Africa.[134] It is submitted that the MDGs are of potential utility for the development of equitable criteria for Article 82 purposes. Recently, States Parties to the Kyoto Protocol established a Climate Change Adaptation Fund to assist developing countries Parties to the Protocol and which are particularly vulnerable to the adverse effects of climate change, to meet the costs of adaptation.[135] The Adaptation Fund will finance "concrete adaptation projects and programmes that are country driven and are based on the needs, views and priorities of eligible Parties."[136] A purpose for payments and contributions could be to supplement the Adaptation Fund to the extent that the eligibility criteria of the Fund are consistent with the equitable criteria developed for Article 82. ICOM is widely recognized as necessary for, *inter alia*, development in coastal zones, avoidance and management of user conflicts, environment and resource protection and planning for natural hazards such as sea level rise, increased storm frequency and floods.[137] With pollution from land-based activities continuing to constitute a major

---

[133] See Michael W. Lodge, "The International Seabed Authority and Article 82 of the United Nations Convention on the Law of the Sea," 21(3) *Int. J. of Mar. & Coast. L.* 323-333 (2006).

[134] United Nations Millennium Declaration, UNGA Resolution 55/2, UN Doc. A/RES/55/2, 18 September 2000.

[135] United Nations Framework Convention on Climate Change, Conference of the Parties serving as the Meeting of the Parties to the Kyoto Protocol, Bali, 3–15 December 2007: Adaptation Fund, Decision 1/CMP.3, UN Doc. FCCC/KP/CMP/2007/9/Add.1, 14 March 2008. The Adaptation Fund Board receives secretariat services from the GEF and the World Bank is interim trustee of the Fund. A review of the interim arrangements for the Fund is expected after three years of operation.

[136] Decision 1/CMP.3, ibid.

[137] This process has been defined as "… a conscious management process that acknowledges the interrelationships among most coastal and ocean uses and the environments they potentially affect. Hence, in a geographical sense, ICM typically embraces upland watersheds, the shoreline and its unique landforms (beaches, dunes, wetlands), nearshore coastal and estuarine waters, and the ocean beyond to the extent it is affected by or affects the coastal area." B. Cicin-Sain and R. Knecht, *Integrated Coastal and Ocean Management: Concepts and Practices* (Washington, D.C.: Island

threat to the marine environment, Agenda 21 (Chapter 17) and the Global Programme of Action for the Protection of the Marine Environment from Land-Based Activities (GPA) prescribed integrated management as the framework for an integrated response to the problem.[138] Another idea is to consider the Common Heritage Fund as a source of support for those developing States which suffer from a major natural disaster in their coastal zones or inland areas (e.g., a tsunami, hurricane/typhoon, seismic activity, or similar event).[139] In this regard, the Climate Change Adaptation Fund mentioned earlier could serve as a model.

Irrespective of the purposes of the benefits and beneficiaries, it is arguable that Article 82 does not necessarily require the Authority to *directly* distribute the benefits itself.[140] Whilst Article 82(4) clearly tasks the Authority with the distribution, there is nothing to suggest that this function may not be delegated, while the Authority retains ultimate responsibility for proper distribution.[141] This course of action can draw upon a precedent in Part XI where the Authority is obligated to "provide for the equitable sharing of financial and other economic benefits derived from activities in the Area through any appropriate mechanism, on a non-discriminatory basis ..."[142] In this scenario, the Authority could avail itself of existing international global and regional mechanisms of the United Nations system. It would need to enter into formal agreements for this purpose. In particular, the United Nations regional economic commissions could be envisaged as channels through which benefits are distributed on a regional basis. There are sound reasons to consider this option. There are appropriate distributive procedures and significant experience in such regional mechanisms. A counter-argument could be the potential cost that might be involved, especially if there is the customary 15 per cent overhead charged for administering trust funds.

Press, 1998), at 1. The Noordwijk Guidelines further define integrated coastal zone management (ICZM) as "a governmental process and consists of the legal and institutional framework necessary to ensure that development and management plans for coastal zones are integrated with environmental (including social) goals and are made with the participation of those affected. The purpose of ICZM is to maximise the benefits provided by the coastal zone and to minimize the conflicts and harmful effects of activities upon each other." The World Bank (Environment Department: Land, Water and Natural Habitats Division), The Noordwijk Guidelines for Integrated Coastal Zone Management, distributed at the World Coast Conference, 1-5 November 1993, Noordwijk, The Netherlands, at 1.

[138] Agenda 21 (in particular Chapter 17). The Programme of Action from Rio (Agenda 21) was adopted at the United Nations Conference on Environment and Development, Rio de Janeiro, 3–14 June 1992; United Nations Division for Sustainable Development, http://www.un.org/esa/sustdev/documents/agenda21/english/agenda21toc.htm; the GPA was adopted at the Intergovernmental Conference to adopt a Global Programme of Action for the Protection of the Marine Environment from Land-Based Activities, Washington, 23 October–3 November 1995, UN Doc. UNEP(OCA)/LBA/IG.2/7, 5 December 1995; United Nations Environment Programme, http://www.gpa.unep.org/documents/full_text_of_the_english.pdf.

[139] HDI Primer, supra note 128, at 46.

[140] Elsewhere in the LOS Convention the use of the term "direct" and its derivatives is expressly stated, e.g.: Arts. 1(4), 19(2)(l), 63(1)&(2), 64(1), 72(1), 123, 161(1)(b), 170(1), 195, 197, 200, 201, 202, 204, 247, 266(1), 268, 269, 271, 275(1), 278. There are similar uses in the annexes of the Convention.

[141] The text "through the Authority" in Article 82(4) simply identifies the administrative function of the Authority in receiving payments and contributions.

[142] LOS Convention, supra note 1, Art. 140(2).

Finally, there is also no indication whether the utilization of the payments and contributions passed on to beneficiaries should be monitored or audited in any way. For example the World Bank monitors country performance. The LOS Convention does not mandate the Authority with this task. It is conceivable that beneficiaries (States in particular) may object to monitoring by an international organization of how they apply the benefits received. The benefits received by virtue of Article 82 will, likely, be viewed as entitlements, not privileges. While it is desirable to have a system of fair distribution according to needs in accordance with the purposes of Article 82 and the Convention as a whole, over-regulation might touch upon political sensitivities and be counter-productive.

6. ISSUES FOR CONSIDERATION IN THE IMPLEMENTATION OF ARTICLE 82

6.1 General

The Article 82 implementation responsibilities of the OCS State and the Authority are intertwined. The OCS State has a legal obligation to make payments and contributions and the Authority has the responsibility to receive these and distribute them on an equitable basis. The Authority's ability to discharge its responsibilities is contingent on receiving the payments or contributions due. Where the obligation is discharged through in-kind contributions, there will conceivably be need for greater dialogue between the two actors, because the Authority might need to make additional arrangements before distribution.

The expectation that there will necessarily be an ongoing relationship between the Authority and OCS States over many years, and the need for effective implementation points to the desirability of having an agreement to govern that relationship within the framework of the LOS Convention. A model "relational agreement," called "Article 82 Agreement" in this report, would facilitate a clear, predictable and efficient relationship conducive to cooperation in the implementation of this provision. Such an agreement would address many of the issues identified in this report. Uniquely among international organizations, the Authority already has extensive experience entering into analogous agreements with LOS Convention States and contractors for exploration of the deep seabed.[143]

Any such Article 82 Agreement would qualify as a treaty under the Vienna Convention on the Law of Treaties between States and International Organizations or between International Organizations, 1986.[144] This convention was adopted under the aegis of the United Nations. Although it is not yet in force, the instrument was developed by the International Law Commission and codifies customary principles and rules for these types of agreements.[145] Intergovernmental organizations may become parties to this convention. The Authority is an intergovernmental organization with full legal

---

[143] For a list of contractors, see International Seabed Authority, http://www.isa.org.jm/en/scientific/ exploration/contractors.

[144] *Vienna Convention on the Law of Treaties between States and International Organizations or between International Organizations*, Vienna, 21 March 1986 (not in force), United Nations Treaty Collection, http://untreaty.un.org/ilc/texts/instruments/english/conventions/1_2_1986.pdf. Thirty-five States Parties are needed to bring this convention into force. At the time of writing there are 30 States Parties that include some OCS States, e.g., Australia, Argentina, Mexico, Spain, UK and Uruguay. Brazil and US have signed the Convention but have not ratified to date.

[145] E.g., conclusion of agreements, entry into force, interpretation, effects, amendments, termination and settlement of disputes. The provisions draw heavily on the 1969 Vienna Convention. Like the Vienna Convention, the 1986 Convention is regarded as codifying the general international principle on the subject. See for example the position of the Executive Board of the World Health Organization: Participation by WHO in the 1986 Vienna Convention on the Law of Treaties between States and International Organizations or between International Organizations: Report by the Secretariat, WHO Doc. EB105/30, 26 October 1999, http://ftp.who.int/gb/archive/pdf_files/ EB105/ee30.pdf.

personality and is thus qualified to become a party. In 1998 the United Nations General Assembly encouraged States and international organizations to become parties to this convention.[146] Although several United Nations agencies are parties, the Authority is not yet a party. Considering the need to enter into Article 82 agreements with OCS States and also agreements with States receiving Article 82 benefits, the Authority might find membership useful.[147]

As was seen earlier, although the basic responsibilities of the OCS State and the Authority are set out explicitly, the text of Article 82 does not provide directions for the *modus operandi*. For the purposes of implementation, it is likely that it will be necessary to infer implicit practical actions to operationalize the provision. These are likely to consist of subsidiary or contingent actions reasonably necessary for the discharge of the respective responsibilities of the OCS State and the Authority. For the Authority, the inferences also relate to the exercise of powers and functions by its organs as set out in relevant Part XI provisions. But there will be a limit to the practical inferences that can be made. For example, it might not be possible to infer the applicable dispute settlement mechanism in the case of differences between the OCS State and the Authority, when the LOS Convention does not provide a mechanism for the resolution of this particular class of dispute. Such a significant omission in the LOS Convention would need to be addressed by agreement between the OCS State and the Authority.

For ease of convenience, in this report the implementation of Article 82 is envisaged to occur over three phases, as set out below and in Annexes I and II:

Phase 1 is a "*pre-production period*" and covers the period of prospecting, exploration and development licences or leases, but before commencement of commercial production. Although there is no production at this stage, the future administrative and fiscal consequences of the OCS royalty will need to be anticipated, especially by the OCS State, because of the long-term spans of non-living resource exploration and exploitation leases, such as those for hydrocarbons and minerals. This period foresees the laying of the foundation for the future "Model Article 82 Agreement".

Phase 2 is the "*grace period*" and concerns the first five years of OCS royalty-free production. This period can be characterized as a "transitional" period during which the producer will be expected to recover most of its costs and the OCS State enjoys a

---

[146] Adopted on 8 December 1998 following proposal by the Sixth Committee. UN General Assembly, United Nations Decade of International Law, UN Doc. A/Res/53/100, 20 January 1999, http://daccessdds.un.org/doc/UNDOC/GEN/N99/762/19/PDF/N9976219.pdf?OpenElement.

[147] Many international organizations are parties: International Atomic Energy Association, International Civil Aviation Organization, International Criminal Police Organization, International Labour Organization, International Maritime Organization, Organization for the Prohibition of Chemical Weapons, Preparatory Commission for the Comprehensive Nuclear Test-Ban Treaty Organization, United Nations, United Nations Industrial Development Organization, Universal Postal Union, World Health Organization and World Intellectual Property Organization. There are other international organizations that have signed but not ratified this convention, e.g.: Food and Agriculture Organization of the United Nations, International Telecommunication Union, United Nations Educational, Scientific and Cultural Organization and World Meteorological Organization. United Nations Treaty Collection, http://treaties.un.org/Pages/ViewDetails.aspx?src=TREATY&mtdsg_no=XXIII-3&chapter=23&lang=en#1 (status as at10 May 2009).

royalty-free period. The development and adoption of the royalty agreement occurs in this phase.

Phase 3 is the "*OCS royalty period*" commencing with the sixth year of production. At this stage the OCS royalty will begin to apply on the scale set out earlier. The duration of this period is coterminous with the commercial life of the non-living resource concerned.

This notional division into phases will now be explored. Although overlapping, the tasks and issues for the OCS State and Authority are set out separately in Annexes I and II because there are several actor-specific matters in each phase. It is possible that the phases (or each phase) will vary from one OCS State to another. However, there are basic tasks within each phase that can be expected to concern all OCS States. Some OCS States might also have other essential tasks not shared by other States and not considered in this report. For example, States with exchange control of foreign currencies might need to legislate authorization for the national government to effect payments under Article 82.

6.2 Tasks and issues for OCS States

6.2.1 Domestic issues for OCS States

At this time it appears that very few OCS States are aware of the significance of Article 82. OCS States need to become aware of the implications of Article 82 when defining the outer limits of their continental shelves and proceeding to offshore exploration and development.

Although the obligation in Article 82 is one at international law and for which the OCS State is responsible, the implementation of that obligation will require the OCS State to determine the level at which the cost discharge will be absorbed. There appears to be three possibilities, and possible combinations of each. The first is for the national government of the OCS State to absorb the payments and contributions and effect payments through the Authority, possibly from royalty and tax revenues levied on production. The second is for the national government to pass the cost on to the producer in the form of additional royalty payments. The OCS State would need to consider the implications of its OCS royalty policy for (a) its existing royalty regime and (b) existing and future concession, production-sharing, service or other contracts, as the case may be. Third, and specifically in the case of States with multiple levels of governance, such as federal States, there might be sub-national governments that could be called upon to share the cost. Sub-national levels of government (e.g., states, provinces, regions) may have rights or expectations from the produced non-living resource. It is possible that a portion or even the bulk of the internal royalties may be enjoyed by sub-national levels of government. They are not bound by Article 82, although they may enjoy royalties under domestic law or political arrangement.[148] Thus, in taking domestic steps

---

[148] For example in Canada, a federal State, the sharing of benefits from offshore resources has long been a contentious legal and political issue. In the case of the two Atlantic provinces of Newfoundland & Labrador and Nova Scotia, the federal and provincial governments federally and provincially

to implement its obligation, the OCS State would need to decide what level (and actor) will bear the cost and how the payments or contributions will be levied.

Although not yet a party to the LOS Convention, the United States, a federal State having a royalty-sharing arrangement with component states, has anticipated how Article 82 will be discharged. As mentioned earlier, the OCS royalty would be levied from producers if the United States becomes a party to the LOS Convention prior to or during the life of a lease.[149] The Lease Stipulations provide for lessees to pay the "Convention-related royalty ... so that the required Convention payments may be made by the U.S. Government as provided under the Convention ..."[150]

Until these issues are determined at the domestic level, industry might perceive uncertainty with respect to Article 82.[151] Industry needs to be engaged at an early stage. It will be important for offshore licensing agencies and legislators in OCS States to clarify for their domestic constituencies the extent to which, if at all, Article 82 payments and contributions will be woven into their royalty regime for the offshore. Industry needs to know, upfront, the tax and royalty conditions of proposed offshore hydrocarbons and mineral resource exploration and development. The United States' practice in this regard indicates one way of doing this. National governments (and sub-national, if applicable) and producers will need to consider commercial viability of OCS fields against the legal realities of development activities on the OCS.

6.2.2 Implementation tasks and issues

(a) Phase 1: Pre-production

Phase 1 is a period during which the OCS State will need to inform itself of the obligation it has to discharge under Article 82 and consider taking a series of anticipatory steps. National policy makers would need to consider whether Article 82 is "within

---

legislated political agreements on the levying of royalties and sharing of revenues, in lieu of continued confrontation. The political agreement reached between Canada and Newfoundland & Labrador allocates the responsibility for the setting and levying of royalties to the province. See Atlantic Accord: Memorandum of Agreement between the Government of Canada and the Government of Newfoundland and Labrador on Offshore Oil and Gas Resource Management and Revenue Sharing, St. John's, Newfoundland, 11 February 1985, Arts. 23 & 37. C-NOPB, http://www.cnlopb.nl.ca/pdfs/guidelines/aa_mou.pdf. The accord's geographical cover includes all of the continental margin adjacent to the province. Ibid., Art. 68. The Accord also provides for the future inclusion of other mineral resources. Ibid., Art. 67.

[149] US Lease Stipulations, supra note 13, Stipulation 4. See Aldo Chircop and Bruce Marchand, "Oceans Act: Uncharted Seas for Offshore Development in Atlantic Canada?" 24 *Dal. L. J.* 23-50 (2001).

[150] Ibid., para. 5. Interestingly, some interests in the United States' oil and gas industry, while considering the obligation as a "modest" revenue-sharing provision, have the understanding that "this royalty should not result in any additional cost to industry." Statement by P. L. Kelly, Senior Vice-President, Rowan Companies, Inc. on behalf of the American Petroleum Institute, International Association of Drilling Contractors and National Ocean Industries Association before the US Senate Committee on Foreign Relations' Hearing on the United Nations Convention on the Law of the Sea, Washington, D.C., 21 October 2003. http://foreign.senate.gov/testimony/2003/KellyTestimony031021.pdf.

[151] Concern has been expressed on the lack of detail on how the revenue-sharing will work. Kelly, ibid.

range", albeit on a long-term horizon. Over a period of years, prior to a resource discovery, the OCS State will be granting prospecting and exploration licences, as the case may be. A development permit is issued in the case of potential commercial discoveries. Although during this period of high risk and cost there is no commercial production, there are tasks to be performed and issues to be anticipated.

The first task is likely to be national policy on Article 82 implementation, namely the course of action the OCS State will want (or should want) to take in discharging its international obligation when it matures. This long-term forecast is essential. As has been seen, licences or leases for the exploration and development of offshore non-living resources have a long-term duration which can span decades. During this phase producers will be assuming significant and costly risk; if there is a commercial discovery there would be even higher costs to bring the discovery into production. The production period is, ostensibly, less costly as the production and transportation infrastructure will be established by then.

The OCS State will have a national energy policy and contracting practices reflecting particular offshore development goals and objectives, and a royalty regime designed to achieve those objectives. For example, the United States lease programme for deep waters in the Gulf of Mexico is motivated by a policy decision to increase domestic oil and gas production to meet national energy needs. They may also have other policies that may be relevant for Article 82 purposes, such as for international development and Kyoto Protocol commitments. OCS States which are listed in Annex 1 of the *United Nations Framework Convention on Climate Change*, 1992 (and *Kyoto Protocol* Annex B) will have to consider the role of OCS resource development in relation to their responsibility to limit greenhouse gas emissions and meet reduction commitments including through the clean development mechanism to assist developing countries in achieving sustainable development.[152] Thus, OCS States will need to consider other costs associated with the development of non-living resources on the OCS, in addition to the making of payments and contributions.

National authorities also will need to anticipate the policy impact of Article 82. Policy harmonization might be necessary, for example where royalty incentives are provided for the taking on of risk in deep-water drilling without consideration of the OCS royalty applicable in the event of production. There will likely be need for consultation with sub-national levels of government (if applicable) and minerals, petroleum and other industries concerned with offshore non-living resources. With regard to the latter, and in a contemporary setting where industry is already taking on risks in OCS areas of some States without reference to the future application of Article 82, industry (especially future producers) might be taking on risk on the understanding that a national (and/or sub-national) production royalty structure without Article 82 would be in place.

The OCS State will, thus, be confronted with the major policy decision as to whether payments and contributions will be absorbed at the national level or some other level.

---

[152] *United Nations Framework Convention on Climate Change*, New York, 9 May 1992, http://unfccc. int/resource/docs/convkp/conveng.pdf; *Kyoto Protocol to the United Nations Framework Convention on Climate Change*, Kyoto, 11 December 1997, Art. 12, http://unfccc.int/resource/docs/convkp/kpeng.pdf.

If the policy choice is for absorption at the national level, a corollary decision relates to whether this action is for defined period(s) or on a permanent basis (i.e., for the duration of the production licence). In the alternative (i.e., that the OCS royalty will not be absorbed at the national level) or where it is absorbed at the national level only for a defined period(s), it would need to be clarified what other level would absorb the cost, whether permanently or for defined period(s). If it is the producers that would absorb the cost, when would the levy (by national or sub-national authorities) of the "OCS royalty" start? In the event that the royalty structure is already in place without consideration of Article 82, would existing royalty rates need to be changed or royalty surcharges imposed? There will be contracts in place and unilateral impositions which diminish the value of the consideration could be skirting on breach or possibly even on expropriation. Should change to the existing royalty structure not be possible, should the OCS State consider grandfathering existing licences? Or, could the fiscal responsibility be shared with a sub-national level, which may well be enjoying the benefits of OCS activity? These can be expected to be politically and legally challenging and potentially costly policy choices.

This complex backdrop should provide sufficient compelling reason for anticipating the implementation of Article 82 at an early stage. Although not a State Party, the United States' repeated practice of announcing the application of the OCS royalty at the Proposed Notice of Lease Sale stage is a sensible practice. Unless it has already made long-term commitments, the OCS State will have time to plan for smooth, cost-effective and cost-equitable implementation. In addition, it would be in a position to plan for an efficient and equitable use of the grace period (Phase 2) as a period of transition. For example, during this period the OCS State might want to design its royalty regime in a manner to enable the producer to recover as much of the costs incurred as possible. As seen earlier, this was the original intention behind the grace period.

Policy change may necessitate concurrent legal and institutional change. For example, the mandates of national authorities responsible for the allocation, administration and monitoring of production licences and receipt of royalty revenues may need to be enlarged to take into consideration in-kind contributions. Additional management and administrative tasks to collect and process payments and contributions may be necessary, such as levying charges on a rising scale in coordination with or as part of the domestic royalty regime(s) and related accounting. A potential concern for the OCS State is the additional institutional and administrative costs that are likely to be incurred in discharging its obligation. As seen earlier, Article 82 does not appear to permit deductions from the payments due to the Authority.

(b)   Phase 2: Grace period

During the first five years of production the OCS State is exempted from making payments or contributions. This is a transitional period for the OCS State and the Authority alike. By now the OCS State should have studied the implementation needs and will have adopted policy directions, as well as taken institutional, administrative and legal measures as necessary. In the meantime, the Authority should have developed policies, rules and regulations for the reception of payments and contributions to provide guidance to OCS States. A number of tasks are foreseen at this stage, culminating in the conclusion of an Article 82 Agreement between the OCS State and the Authority.

At first, the OCS State will need to provide the Authority with notice of the prospective application of the obligation. Although the provision of notice of prospective production is not an explicit requirement in Article 82, it is an action which can reasonably be inferred from the obligation to make payments or contributions through the Authority. Ideally, although this is not current OCS State practice, the Authority should receive formal notice from OCS States that they are opening up lease areas on the OCS and calling for bids, and eventually granting exploration licences. The Authority will need to know when the obligation is expected to commence because it will need to take the steps necessary to discharge its own responsibilities. Reading a notice requirement into Article 82 is, thus, both reasonable and practical.

The production notice would need to be provided during Phase 2 because the payment or contribution is determined from the date of commencement of production. At a minimum, the OCS State should inform the Authority of the particular site, official date of commencement of commercial production and the type of non-living resource concerned. The site, i.e., the location of the resource must be communicated to the Authority (i.e., production occurring from a site on the OCS State's continental shelf), because it is conceivable that there might be other sites to be brought into production in the same lease round.

In the hypothetical scenario of the non-living resource straddling a neighbouring EEZ, the OCS or perhaps the Area, and especially if the development of the resource is unitized, it is conceivable that the amount of payment or contribution due from the OCS State may be affected, or may need to be calculated on the basis of the respective shares enjoyed by concerned States. The Authority itself would have an interest in production activities from a mineral resource straddling the Area and the payment or contribution would need to reflect only the amount of production on the neighbouring OCS site.

In this phase, the OCS State should also notify the Authority of its choice between making payments or contributions in kind. Because the obligation has to be discharged on an annual basis and based on the amount of production, the OCS State will need to effect the first payment or contribution towards the end of the sixth year of production or at a reasonable time shortly thereafter. The Authority will need to be informed of the precise details during Phase 2. For example, if the obligation will be discharged through payments, the Authority will need to know the currency and amounts of payments, and the fiscal year or period used as a basis for "annual" payments. Although not stated for Article 82, the LOS Convention provides for the currency of the budget and transactions of the Authority, and in an ideal scenario the Authority and the OCS State will discharge their respective responsibilities on the basis of this currency. Calculating the payment due could be an accounting issue for the OCS State because any of the produced resource utilised to enhance production is not to be included in the determination of total production.

The OCS State enjoys discretion in choosing to make in-kind contributions and will need to inform the Authority accordingly. Ideally, the OCS State should consult the Authority on in-kind contributions because particular arrangements may need to be made by the Authority to receive the contemplated contributions.

For States (especially developed) the making of Article 82 payments or contributions should not be characterised as delivering on their official development assistance (ODA) commitments under the Monterrey Consensus or other international commitments.[153] Article 82 establishes a separate obligation from international ODA commitments OCS States might make.

In the case the OCS royalty is levied from the producer, and unless already anticipated in Phase 1, the impact on existing contracting practices (e.g., concessions, production-sharing, service agreements, etc.) has to be addressed. An appropriate domestic collection and accounting procedure would need to be in place by the end of the grace period.

(c) Phase 3: OCS royalty

Phase 3 commences with the sixth year of production and when the OCS Royalty matures. In order for the OCS State to determine the annual amounts due, it will need to determine actual total production for the first and subsequent years in order to determine value or volume, as the case may be. It will deduct amounts of the resource in question used in connection with production. Subsequently, it will need to effect the payments or contributions. This may begin at the end of the production year but could, foreseeably and reasonably, spill over into the following year because the total production might not be fully accounted for by the end of the year. This likelihood has been foreseen by the US Lease Stipulations which provide for OCS royalty payment to be made on or before 30 days after expiration of the relevant production lease year.[154] This exercise of determining the value or volume of payments or contributions would then continue on a regular annual basis. It is conceivable that unexpected changes to total production which are likely to affect the amount of payments or contributions may occur, for example, because offshore activities may need to be temporarily closed because of bad weather, a *force majeure* situation, or because of fluctuating market conditions. This report suggests that a duty to inform is reasonable for such situations. The OCS State should notify the Authority of such unexpected changes in the likelihood that the Authority's ability to discharge its own Article 82 implementation responsibilities is affected.

Again, there are potential issues for the OCS State in this phase. Clearly, the Authority will need to receive information from the OCS State to enable it to discharge

---

[153] The commitment by developed countries to provide ODA up to 0.7% of GDP goes back to a UN General Assembly resolution in 1970: "In recognition of the special importance of the role that can be fulfilled only by official development assistance, a major part of financial resource transfers to the developing countries should be provided in the form of official development assistance. Each economically advanced country will progressively increase its official development assistance to the developing countries and will exert its best efforts to reach a minimum net amount of 0.7 percent of its gross national product at market prices by the middle of the decade." Restated on several occasions, this was reiterated more recently in the "Monterrey Consensus," see Report of the International Conference on Financing for Development Monterrey, Mexico, 18–22 March 2002, UN Doc. A/CONF.198/11 (New York: United Nations, 2002), http://www.unmillenniumproject.org/documents/07_aconf198-11.pdf.

[154] US Lease Stipulations, supra note 13, para. 9.

its responsibilities. The question that arises is how much technical, economic and management information the Authority needs to properly discharge its responsibilities. Such information may be not only proprietary but also commercially sensitive. In providing such information, the OCS State may well need the Authority to commit to a confidentiality protocol, possibly as a term in the Article 82 Agreement. Determination of the well-head value for hydrocarbons, or analogous value for minerals at a time of fluctuating commodity market prices could also be an issue. The Article 82 Agreement could provide a formula for the determination of value.

In the event the OCS State opts for in-kind contributions, the delivery of the contributions could pose an issue. The making of in-kind contributions in the form of a share of the resource produced could entail shipping or pipeline transportation arrangements. This is potentially an issue for both the OCS State and the Authority because, as has been seen, Article 82 does not explicitly permit deduction of costs from the payments or contributions made and received. This is a very different scenario from the MMS when receiving RIK and the arrangements and related costs should be addressed in the Article 82 Agreement.

6.3 Tasks and issues for the Authority

6.3.1 Role of the Authority

Other than a role in Article 82(4) and responsibilities for the Assembly and Council in Part XI, there is little guidance on how the Authority might perform its functions to facilitate the implementation of Article 82 and achieve its overall purposes.[155] Article 82 is outside Part XI, within which the Authority is established and whose general functions are mostly set out with reference to that part of the Convention. This situation calls for a more in-depth consideration of the role and tasks of the Authority in this regard and the powers and functions it has or needs to have in order to perform tasks. The role to be played by the Authority will need to be inferred in part by reference to the express text of Article 82 itself and its negotiating history, in part by reference to other express provisions in the Convention, and also with reference to what may be implicitly inferred from the tasks allocated to it in Article 82 to enable the achievement of the objects and purposes of this provision. The exercise of setting out the role the Authority will need to play has to proceed with caution to ensure that it reflects the letter and spirit of the applicable provisions of the LOS Convention.[156]

---

[155] During its ten-year period of working to prepare the structures and processes to facilitate the implementation of key institutions established by the LOS Convention, especially the ISA, PrepCom was not expressly tasked to consider the Article 82 role of the Authority. Within the LOS Convention and the mandate given to it at the end of UNCLOS III, PrepCom produced various recommendations, rules, procedures, agreements and studies, *inter alia* for the organs of the Authority, and for the purposes of this report the Assembly and Council. The bulk of the work focused on structures and processes that would enable the ISA to function without delay once the Convention came into force, but none focused on the Article 82 responsibility. Final Act of UNCLOS III, Annex I, Resolution I: Establishment of the Preparatory Commission for the International Sea-Bed Authority and for the International Tribunal for the Law of the Sea, LOS Convention, supra note 1, pp. 175–176.

[156] "With respect to the proposal to carry out a study of the implications of article 82, paragraph 4, of

The Authority has an "international legal personality and such legal capacity as may be necessary for the exercise of its functions and the fulfillment of its purposes."[157] The Authority is provided with powers and functions in relation to Article 82 responsibilities not in the text of that provision, but rather in Part XI. As the supreme organ of the Authority, the Assembly is empowered "to establish general policies in conformity with the relevant provisions of this Convention on any question or matter within the competence of the Authority."[158] As the Authority's executive organ, the Council is empowered to establish specific policies on any matter within the Authority's competence, but within the more general policies of the Assembly.[159] More specifically, the Council is empowered to "... recommend to the Assembly rules, regulations and procedures on the equitable sharing of financial and other economic benefits derived from activities in the Area and the payments and contributions made pursuant to Article 82, taking into particular consideration the interests and needs of developing States and peoples who have not attained full independence or other self-governing status ..."[160] In turn, the Assembly will consider the Council's recommendations and may approve them or "return them to the Council for reconsideration in the light of the views expressed by the Assembly."[161]

Given the lack of detail on the role of the Authority in Article 82(4), what functions can be considered implicit and consistent with the nature of its role in this provision, and perhaps even essential for the performance of this task? As a treaty-creation, the Authority is required to exercise powers and functions within the framework and boundaries of its empowering instrument, which "shall be those expressly conferred upon it by this Convention."[162] However, the Authority "shall have such incidental powers, consistent with this Convention, as are implicit in and necessary for the exercise of those powers and functions with respect to activities in the Area."[163] The incidental powers seem to be with reference to activities in the Area, whereas Article 82 is unrelated to activities in the Area. Although Article 82 is established outside Part XI, the Authority's role in this article is also expressly referred to in the powers and functions of the organs of the Authority in Part XI, namely in Articles 160(2)(f)(i) and 162(2)(o)(i). The interpretation of Article 82(4) needs to be tied to the general powers and functions of the Authority in Part XI, because it is through the exercise of these powers and functions that the Authority will be able to facilitate the achievement of the objects and purposes of that provision.

---

the LOS Convention, some delegations expressed the view that the responsibilities of the Authority under article 82 were strictly limited to the functions set out in article 82, paragraph 4, and that any study by the secretariat should be focused accordingly." As reported in "Statement of the President on the Work of the Assembly at the Ninth Session," Assembly, Ninth Session, Kingston, Jamaica, 28 July– 8 August 2002, ISBA/9/A/9, 7 August 2003. See also "Seabed Assembly Discusses Secretary-General's Annual Report," ISA Press Release, SB/9/12, 5 August 2003.

[157] LOS Convention, supra note 1, Art. 176.
[158] Ibid., Art. 160(1).
[159] Ibid., Art. 162(1).
[160] Ibid., Art. 162(2)(o)(i).
[161] Ibid., Art. 160(2)(f)(i).
[162] Ibid., Art. 157(2).
[163] Ibid.

A few examples will help illustrate the need to infer implicit functions. First, corollary to the OCS State's obligation to make payments or contributions is the Authority's duty to distribute these to States Parties. The Authority is, in effect, acting upon the interests of States Parties in receiving the payments or contributions. It is reasonable to interpret this responsibility as including an implicit subsidiary function for the Authority to monitor and determine when payments and contributions are due. Second, it is difficult to envisage a situation where the Authority, in receiving payments for example, might not also hold on to those monies temporarily and until their distribution to States Parties. If this is a reasonably foreseeable scenario, the consequence is that the Authority might well have an implicit fiduciary responsibility, possibly as a trustee.[164] Third, whereas the Authority has an express mandate to distribute the payments and contributions to States Parties on the basis of equitable sharing criteria, the provision does not indicate the criteria applicable for this purpose. Again, given the express distributive task given to the Authority, it is reasonable to suggest that this provision implicitly tasks the Authority with the development of these criteria so as to be able to achieve the objects and purposes of the provision.

6.3.2 Implementation tasks and issues

(a)   Phase 1: Pre-production

The Authority should undertake a number of preliminary tasks in Phase 1. In particular, it would need to determine the full extent of its responsibilities in Article 82 and the powers and functions it may use for those purposes. As indicated earlier, the sparse explicit responsibilities may need to be accompanied by an interpretation of implicit functions reasonably necessary to enable it to discharge its mandate. This should include the scope of the Council's powers and functions to make rules, regulations and procedures in Article 160(2)(o)(i) and to take any action to secure compliance with its rules, regulations and procedures.

Clarification of explicit and implicit responsibilities, powers and functions is a prelude to policy development. The Council would need to develop a policy for the implementation of Article 82 to submit to the Assembly for its consideration and adoption. Issues to be considered at this stage include the extent to which policies, rules, procedures and processes developed or that will be developed for activities in the Area can be transposed to the Authority's responsibilities in Article 82 and formulation of equitable criteria for distribution of benefits. The latter should include formulation of appropriate goals for the distribution of payments and contributions (e.g., to assist

---

[164] Presumably pursuant to Regulation 5.5 of the Financial Regulations of the International Seabed Authority, which authorize the ISA Secretary-General to establish trust funds and special accounts. Financial Regulations of the Authority in *International Seabed Authority: Basic Texts* (Kingston, Jamaica: International Seabed Authority, 2003) [hereafter Financial Regulations], 87-98, at 90. It is not clear how Article 82 revenues will be classed. Regulation 7.1 simply states that Article 82 payments will not be classed as miscellaneous income for credit to the general administrative fund. Ibid., 92–93.

adaptation to climate change related response and mitigation strategies, assist integrated coastal and ocean management, etc.).[165]

Within the overall policy framework, the Authority would need to adopt policies, rules, regulations and procedures and develop an administrative structure to receive payments and contributions in kind. Its efforts in this regard would need to include a monitoring, accounting and auditing system for incoming payments and contributions and disbursements to beneficiaries. It is likely that the Authority will either need to enhance its expertise in oil and gas and mineral resources law, resource economics and accounting, and related areas by hiring expert personnel or by outsourcing its knowledge needs to well-established and experienced consulting firms in those fields.

In order to minimize the demand to enhance institutional capacity and related costs, the Authority should consider entering into arrangements with OCS States, seeking their assistance to liquidate any in-kind contributions into a convertible currency. There would be a cost attached to this. In this way the Authority will only need to manage "payments", a significantly less demanding exercise than having to make arrangements for in-kind contributions

To help assist OCS States, in particular developing OCS States, in the discharge of their obligations and standardize the procedures for payments and contributions, the Authority should consider adopting guidelines to assist the domestic implementation of Article 82 and the process of effecting payments and contributions. Ideally, guidelines should be formally made available to OCS States well in advance of Article 82 becoming operational. Different guidelines may be needed with respect to the various non-living resources captured by Article 82. The development of guidelines should be undertaken in consultation with interested OCS and other States. The process of developing guidelines will constitute an opportunity to conduct much needed capacity-building. The guidelines could address a range of matters including: the nature of the obligation in Article 82 and the options and related responsibilities of the OCS State, standard definitions (e.g., site, value, volume, production, etc.); defining the starting point of production for royalty purposes; the scale of payments and contributions and how they might be calculated consistently with Article 82; information on the Model Article 82 Agreement; the notices that should be given to the Authority by the OCS State and the information that, ideally, should be contained therein; recommendations concerning situations which might interrupt production and consequent payments and contributions in kind and for which the OCS State should give notice to the Authority, and so on.

The royalty is due only as long as there is production. Should production be interrupted, a question arises as to the consequence for the continued calculation of the scale of payments. The key question is whether the clock stops running as long as the interruption, especially in a *force majeure* scenario, persists. In the interests of equity, it is not unreasonable to expect that the clock stops running for as long as the interruption persists. The time frames in the scale of payments and contributions would have to be adjusted accordingly. But it is also reasonable to expect the coastal State to

---

[165] It is possible that the Authority might interpret its mandate in a manner that requires endorsement by States Parties to the LOS Convention (SPLOS) or perhaps an advisory opinion from ITLOS.

give formal notice of the commencement and termination of such occurrence, and in the absence of which the normal schedule of payments and contributions would continue. This scenario should be addressed in the Article 82 Agreement.

At this point, the Authority should anticipate the OCS States likely to be first engaged by Article 82 and identify national contact points. Over time, the Authority would want to monitor OCS activities around the world that might become Article 82 eligible.

The Authority will need to consider the costs to be expected to enable it to implement Article 82 responsibilities and seek the advice and directions from its member States. As indicated earlier, the LOS Convention does not authorise the Authority to recover its costs from the payments and contributions made. Whether the Authority's budget for Article 82 distributions should be kept separate from the regular budget for Part XI activities will need to be considered. The Finance Committee of the Authority is empowered to make recommendations that could include funding for the administration of Article 82 responsibilities.[166]

(b) Phase 2: Grace period

In Phase 2 the Authority will need to acknowledge receipt of notices from an OCS State concerning the prospective application of the obligation in its regard, commencement of production and the option to make payments or contributions.

The Authority will need to take administrative steps to be ready to receive payments or contributions. As indicated earlier, entering into an Article 82 Agreement would be a useful tool for an efficient relationship which will involve regular payments and contributions. For this purpose the Authority should develop a model agreement which, while having a common core for all OCS States, would also have the flexibility to adapt to the particular situation of an OCS State, the resource concerned and the option it chooses. Consultation of OCS States and involvement of experts from those and other States will be needed to develop standard terms in the model agreement. The Authority should enter into Article 82 Agreements with eligible States during Phase 2.

In anticipation of its distributive assignment, the Authority will need to develop equitable criteria for eligibility and distribution of the payments and contributions. It will need to adopt rules, regulations and procedures and have these approved by member States. The development of equitable criteria will not be a simple process and, as indicated earlier, it is likely that an appropriate composite index for the ranking of beneficiaries would need to be created. It would also need to determine the procedure for the distribution of benefits and set out related safeguards. The Authority might also consider developing a model agreement as a vehicle for the distribution of benefits.

Internally, the Authority will need to allocate to the Council the task to develop equitable criteria. Although the Authority's tasks in Article 82 can also be described as "financial," the Finance Committee has not been empowered to be engaged in the making of rules, regulations and procedures for Article 82, as in the case of the Council and Assembly. The Finance Committee's tasks appear to be focused on the functioning

---

[166] Part XI Agreement, Annex, Section 9, para. 7(c), in Compendium, supra note 1, 86.

of the Authority and the benefits from the Area. In fact, it is composed of contributing States (i.e., to the Authority), but not beneficiary States. As indicated earlier, the Finance Committee is likely to play a role in determining the costs of the Authority's implementation responsibilities for Article 82 and, potentially, also to recommend administrative procedures for the distribution of payments and contributions.

The development of equitable criteria is more likely a task that will more appropriately be undertaken by the Legal and Technical Commission in an advisory capacity to the Council, because it appears to have been expressly so tasked by the LOS Convention.[167] It is arguable that the Economic Planning Commission, although not expressly tasked by the LOS Convention with Article 82 responsibilities, has the appropriate composition (including expertise in international trade or economics) and substantive functions (in particular advice provided to the Council concerning a system of compensation or other measures of economic adjustment for developing States affected by activities in the Area) that are closest to the expertise needed for the development of equitable criteria.[168] However, at this time the Economic Planning Commission is not in existence and its functions are being performed by the Legal and Technical Commission until such time as the Council decides otherwise or the first plan of work for exploitation is approved.[169]

(c)   Phase 3: OCS royalty

In this phase the tasks of the Authority will, essentially, be administrative in terms of receiving payments and contributions, acknowledging receipt of these and distributing them to States Parties. The Authority will be engaged in relational agreements and will have to maintain working relationships with OCS States and their designated counterpart authorities, and States designated as beneficiaries on the basis of application of equitable criteria developed in the earlier phase. The composite index for the distribution of benefits in accordance with equitable criteria will need to be reviewed on a regular basis as socio-economic circumstances change. The Authority will likely face challenges in managing fluctuating values of payments and contributions in kind as a result of fluctuations in currency values and commodity prices.

---

[167] LOS Convention, supra note 1, Art. 165(2)(f). Although not material to this report, this provision suffers from imprecise drafting. It empowers the Legal and Technical Commission to formulate and submit rules, regulations and procedures to the Council referred to in Art. 162(2)(o), without distinguishing between sub-paragraphs (o)(i) and (o)(ii). Sub-paragraph (o)(i) concerns Art. 82 and (ii) relates to regulations concerning activities in the Area. A more precise drafting of the Commission's task in relation to both (i) and (ii) should have kept the two regulatory functions separate. This is so because the proviso in 165(2)(f) "taking into account all relevant factors including assessments of the environmental implications of activities in the Area" clearly cannot apply to Art. 82.

[168] Ibid., Art. 164(1) and (2)(d).

[169] Part XI Implementation Agreement, supra note 24, Annex, Section 1, para. 4.

6.4 Non-living resources straddling the limits of the OCS

6.4.1 Stating the issue

The implementation of Article 82 in the context of OCS non-living resources straddling maritime zone limits or boundaries raises additional questions relating to: (a) the determination of the amount of payment or contribution in kind with respect to a site in a qualifying OCS area, and (b) the cooperation needed in a situation where exploitation activities on an OCS site concern non-living resources that straddle the Area. Article 82(2) refers to "production at a site" as the basis for calculation of payments and contributions due.

The negotiation history of Article 82 does not indicate whether production from a site located in a non-OCS area and which includes non-living resources located in the adjacent OCS was included within the ambit of the provision. This scenario is conceivable where that part of the resource located on the OCS is accessed from the non-OCS area through directional drilling or where a fugacious resource migrates in the reservoir to the extraction point. The negotiation of this provision seems to have assumed that "a site" simply referred to the OCS location of the exploitation of the non-living resource. In other words, the exploitation of resources belonging to other seabed and subsoil areas (i.e., other than OCS areas) could not be captured by Article 82, irrespective of the location from where they are exploited. This speaks to common sense when cross-referred to Article 77(1): sovereign rights are exercised by the coastal State over the continental shelf "for the purpose of exploring *it* and exploiting *its* resources" (emphasis added). The possessive pronoun suggests there should be a narrow reading relating to the spatial origins of the non-living resource produced, and is again used in paragraph (2) of the Article. A consequential reading of "site" with reference to the compromise reached between Articles 76 (definition of the continental shelf) and 82 suggests that "site" should be interpreted with reference to resources located on the OCS as defined in accordance with the LOS Convention. If "site" is read to include exploitation of resources located outside the OCS, the compromise reached would be defeated. Similarly, and consistently with this interpretation, exploitation of OCS resources from outside the OCS would be captured by Article 82.[170]

Assuming that the above is a correct interpretation of "site," a further consideration is the calculation of payments and contributions with respect to production of a resource that may straddle the limits of the OCS. With regard to (a) there are four potential scenarios:

(1) the OCS resource straddles the EEZ of the OCS State;
(2) the OCS resource straddles the EEZ of a neighbouring State;
(3) the OCS resource straddles the OCS of a neighbouring OCS State; and
(4) the OCS resource straddles the Area.

The first three will be considered together below. Scenario (4) also concerns (a) and will be considered separately below. However, before proceeding further, it is useful to

---

[170] Conversely, an EEZ resource exploited from the OCS would not be captured by Article 82.

provide a brief comment on the common practice of "unitization" in the development and production of a "fugacious" resource, specifically oil and gas.[171] When a resource reservoir underlies more than one licence area, it is likely that the resource requires development across the licence boundary.[172] The necessity stems from the likely wasteful alternative of competitive drilling and production otherwise possible under the rule of capture. The principle and practice of unitization attempts to take an integrated approach to the development of the resource to maximize production and reduce inefficiencies. It implies that the placement of production units would be strategic to achieve this purpose, irrespective of boundaries. The production "site," consisting of multiple and strategically placed installations, would thus be transboundary. Typically, the respective licence holders would address the issue as a private law matter, although national or sub-national legislation may also require them to cooperate.[173]

6.4.2 Production from a site concerning non-living resources straddling maritime zone limits or boundaries

Where (1) occurs, the producing State would need to determine what percentage of the production is proportionate to that part of the resource located on the OCS. An OCS State does not necessarily delineate offshore areas for development (including licensing) to coincide with the EEZ outer limit (see the practice of Canada in Figure 1 above). Yet, identifying the source of the resource produced is necessary because only that part of the production relating to OCS resources would be subject to payments or contributions, even though the resource would be developed as a unit. This could

---

[171] "Unitization is the joint, coordinated operation of a petroleum reservoir by all the owners of rights in the separate tracts overlying the reservoir." Licence holders typically enter into a joint operating agreement. Jacqueline Lang Weaver and David Asmus, "Unitizing Oil and Gas Fields Around the World: A Comparative Analysis of National Laws and Private Contracts," 28(3) *Houston J.I.L.* (2006), http://papers.ssrn.com/sol3/papers.cfm?abstract_id=900645. See also: "International Unitization of Oil and Gas Fields: the Legal Framework of International Law, National Laws, and Private Contracts," 2 *Oil, Gas & Energy L. J.* (2007), Unitization and JDZs; J. C. Woodliffe, "International Unitization of an Offshore Gas Field," 26 *I.C.L.Q.* 338-353 (1977).

[172] Lang and Asmus advise, as a matter of good practice, that a statute, regulation or model contract should "allow unitization of more than one field, strata, or reservoir." supra note 171, at 60.

[173] On international practice, see Lang and Asmus, ibid., at 22 et seq. In the US almost all states "have compulsory unitization statutes which authorize their conservation commissions to order unwilling owners to join the unit on a basis approved after notice and hearing before the commission." Ibid., at 18. Similar regulation applies to offshore development, which clearly concerns federal lands. "Lessees often unitize at the development stage to allow rational development of very expensive prospects. It is often not feasible to separately develop two offshore blocks using two separate platforms and pipelines, given the enormous capital expenditures required." Ibid., at 20. The MMS "allows voluntary unitization but can require unitization where it deems such unitization to be necessary to prevent waste, conserve natural resources, or protect correlative rights. Units in the offshore United States may encompass many blocks with separate ownership by different lessees to allow use of common facilities; separate participating areas are formed to address sharing of costs and production for each reservoir that crosses lease boundaries." Ibid. The Association of International Petroleum Negotiators (AIPN) has developed a Model Form International Operating Agreement. AIPN, http://www.aipn.org/modelagreements/.

be a complex exercise because the extraction of the resource in a particular location might not necessarily be proportionate to the field as a whole. It is conceivable that more of the resource can be extracted from one part of the field than from another. Further, although the producer is incurring costs, it is only the gross production from the OCS area that will be subject to payments and contributions. Difficulties could be exacerbated at the domestic level where some producers would be subject to the OCS royalty levy, but not others. For example, producers within the 200M limit would not have to pay such a levy. The OCS State might need to consider whether it would need to compensate operators for this uneven playing field, and potentially it could result in lower revenues for that State from OCS activities.

In the case of (2) and (3), presumably the development of the transboundary resource will be unitized as a matter of good practice. The scenario of a transboundary single geological structure or non-living resources straddling an international maritime boundary has been considered in bilateral treaty practice and international judicial and arbitral decisions. For decades, numerous bilateral continental shelf and other maritime boundary agreements anticipated the possibility of discovery of single geological structures across maritime boundaries and provided for bilateral cooperation between those neighbouring States.[174] For example, in the North Sea neighbouring Norway and the United Kingdom have long cooperated on the joint development of the transboundary Frigg and Statfjord fields using unitization principles, foreseen in their continental shelf boundary agreement.[175] There are also numerous examples of joint development zones, frequently complex arrangements between States that similarly addressed the joint development needs of transboundary resources.[176] International judicial and arbitral decisions have also encouraged joint cooperative approaches to transboundary marine resource development as provisional measures, including where there are boundary disputes.

In this scenario Article 82 will apply to the OCS portion only in the case of (2) and to the overall production from the unitized field or joint development zone in the case of (3). In the case of (3) the neighbouring OCS States would have to agree on their respective shares of payments or contributions, just as much as they would normally agree on benefit-sharing. On the other hand, if the development is unilateral, then the payment or contribution is clearly the duty of the producing State only.

6.4.3 Production from a site concerning non-living resources straddling the outer limits of the OCS and the Area

In the case of (4), there could be two scenarios. The first is one where the OCS State undertakes unilateral development of the transboundary resource, in which case

---

[174] In particular in relation to continental shelf boundary agreements. For examples of such agreements and other cooperative arrangements in the context of maritime boundaries on a marine regional basis, see *International Maritime Boundaries* vols. I-V (various eds.) (Leiden: Brill, 1993-2005).

[175] Woodliffe, supra note 171.

[176] See *International Maritime Boundaries*, supra note 174.

it would have to make the payment or contribution in relation to production from its OCS.[177] The second scenario is where the Authority enters into a joint development arrangement with the OCS State. In this case there would have to be agreement on what proportion of the production is subject to payments and contributions. In this scenario, the rules and procedures for the exploration and exploitation of the Area in Part XI would come into play, although the Authority's jurisdiction would be limited to those activities specifically occurring in the Area.[178]

With regard to (b), the major concern for the Authority is a scenario (4) where the OCS State undertakes exploitation of a transboundary fugacious resource on a unilateral basis and through activities located on the OCS alone, such as directional drilling. This concern is more of an issue for the Authority's Part XI mandate and related responsibilities on behalf of mankind than for the administration of Article 82. However, there could be an indirect Article 82 issue because payments and contributions relate to the exploitation of the non-living resources of the OCS. In this scenario, through directional drilling the OCS State might have access to resources located in the Area, without resorting to Part XI procedures, and will likely be a treaty violation.

Although potentially not consistent with good oilfield practice, this scenario is conceivable, although unlikely. An OCS State embarking on such conduct risks the political cost of protest, if not opposition, by other LOS Convention member States who would justifiably perceive such conduct to occur at the expense of the common heritage of mankind. The OCS State might argue the rule of capture in its favour. However, this is tenuous, at best. The classical rule of capture in the common law held that the resource is "owned" when captured, i.e., it is brought to the surface.[179] There have been modifications to this old rule because it was considered to carry undesirable social costs, and was inconsistent with resource conservation principles and good oilfield practice.[180] Unitization is the acceptable practice in a contemporary context, so that the location of extractive activities is with reference to the best possible location to maximize resource development, irrespective of jurisdiction. Fortunately, the rule of capture is not a principle or rule of international law.[181]

---

[177] The Convention does not appear to provide a duty on the OCS State to consult the ISA on the development of transboundary resources (straddling the OCS and the Area), although there may be one at customary law. For a discussion on this topic, see David M. Ong, "Joint Development of Common Offshore Oil and Gas Deposits: 'Mere' State Practice or Customary International Law?" 93 *A.J.I.L.* 771 (1999). There is, however, a duty on the ISA to act with due regard to the rights and legitimate interests of the OCS State. The duty requires consultation, including prior notification. See LOS Convention, supra note 1, Art. 142. On the basis of *Suriname/Guyana*, the Authority would probably have a reasonable expectation to be informed, consulted and invited to cooperate by the OCS State in relation to a non-living resource straddling the OCS and the Area which the OCS State intends to develop. *Suriname/Guyana*, Permanent Court of Arbitration (Award), 17 September 2007, http://www.pca-cpa.org/showpage.asp?pag_id=1147.

[178] LOS Convention, supra note 1, Art. 153.

[179] Bruce M. Kramer and Owen L. Andersen, "The Rule of Capture: An Oil and Gas Perspective," 35 *Env. L.* 899-954 (2005), at 900-901.

[180] Kramer and Andersen, ibid.

[181] Dominic Roughton, "The Rights (and Wrongs) of Capture: International Law and the Implications of the Guyana/Suriname Arbitration" (Tokyo: Herbert Smith LLP in association with Gleiss Lutz and Stibbe, undated).

A further question is whether the body of treaty and judicial practice on this matter, which is exclusively directed at bilateral relations between neighbouring States, is of assistance to the Authority as an intergovernmental organization with responsibilities in the Area (beyond national jurisdiction) and as a putative "neighbour" to the OCS State. This report argues that the analogy is useful as (i) unitization is good practice irrespective of the location of the resource, and (ii) the general purpose of cooperative transboundary resource arrangements is to ensure efficiency and equity between neighbours. Although falling outside the terms of reference of this report, the Authority might wish to consider a cooperative transboundary resource arrangement with OCS States in this scenario. This would likely facilitate its ability to discharge both Part XI and Article 82 responsibilities.

7. THE RESOLUTION OF ARTICLE 82 DISPUTES

As has been pointed out, the LOS Convention stipulates an obligation for States Parties to fulfill in their obligations in good faith and not to exercise their rights in a manner which amounts to an abuse of right. The Convention is silent on the consequences of lack of good faith, abuse of right or a direct violation in relation to Article 82.[182] There is also the hypothetical possibility that a State Party might question the Authority's exercise of its powers and functions with regard to Article 82.

During UNCLOS III the Group of Land-Locked and Geographically Disadvantaged States anticipated the potential issue of an OCS State violating its Article 82 obligation. The Group suggested that the Authority be empowered to take appropriate measures consistently with its powers and functions.[183] The concern included determining when a default in the making of payments or contributions occurred. There was no consensus on the inclusion of this proposal in the Convention.

In Part XV the LOS Convention establishes an elaborate dispute settlement framework, providing a range of options for the resolution of the wide diversity of disputes that can arise within the context of the instrument. While States Parties have access to most of the dispute settlement options, the Authority has much more limited access to that framework.[184]

Access to that framework is further limited by the jurisdictional constraints imposed by the Convention. The Authority has access to the Seabed Disputes Chamber of the International Tribunal for the Law of the Sea (ITLOS) when the claim concerns eligible subject-matter.[185] There are two issues of concern. The first is that *prima facie* the general description of the jurisdiction of the Chamber to entertain disputes appears to be spatially restricted (*ratione loci*) to disputes with respect to "activities in the Area" (Article 187). Second, as an institution established by treaty, the ITLOS (consequently also the Chamber) is a judicial institution with limited jurisdiction. The general description of its jurisdiction is further limited by subject-matter (*ratione materiae*). The scope of that jurisdiction is itemized in Article 187, and the heads of jurisdiction (categories of disputes) specified therein do not include Article 82 matters.[186]

A dispute concerning the Authority's exercise of its powers and functions in Articles 160(2)(f)(i) and 162(2)(o)(i) (i.e., through the Assembly and/or Council) raises two further considerations. First, and to the disadvantage of the Authority, it does not concern "activities in the Area." Second, and to the disadvantage of the OCS State, the

---

[182] For example where an OCS State refuses to make, or unreasonably delays, or is erratic in the making of the required payments or contributions.

[183] See Informal Single Negotiating Text II (ISNT II), Art. 69(5) proposed by the group of Land-Locked and Geographically Disadvantaged States: "If a State concerned fails to comply with the provisions of this article the International Authority may take appropriate measures in accordance with the powers and functions conferred upon it by this Convention." Platzöder, supra note 27, Vol. IV, 327.

[184] "The dispute settlement procedures specified in this Part [i.e., Part XV on dispute settlement] shall be open to entities other than States Parties only as specifically provided for in this Convention." LOS Convention, supra note 1, Art. 291(2).

[185] Ibid., Art. 187 and Annex VI, Art. 37.

[186] Ibid., Art. 187. An Art. 82 interpretation or implementation dispute is not encompassed by "activities in the Area."

competence of the Chamber to pronounce itself on the dispute and provide appropriate remedies is further limited.[187] The Chamber is required to defer to the Authority's decision-making, including whether decisions are *intra* or *ultra vires*: it "shall not pronounce itself on the question of whether any rules, regulations and procedures of the Authority are in conformity with this Convention, nor declare invalid any such rules, regulations and procedures."[188]

Part XV is concerned with disputes between States, as well as Part XI Section 5 disputes, including "such a dispute" involving an entity other than a State Party.[189] Despite the intention of the negotiators of UNCLOS III to extend the application of Part XV Section 1 to disputes between a State Party and the Authority,[190] the technical reference to "such a dispute" (i.e., disputes pursuant to Part XI, Section 5, i.e., re "activities in the Area" and the heads of jurisdiction identified therein), seems to exclude Article 82 disputes.

While arriving to the same conclusion concerning the limitations of the Part XV dispute settlement procedures concerning Article 82 disputes, the ILA Report mentioned earlier makes two additional observations that should be highlighted.[191] The first points to the Article 191 power of the Assembly and Council to seek an advisory opinion from the Chamber "on legal questions arising within the scope of their activities." As seen earlier, Article 82(4) and the powers and functions set out in Articles 160(2)(f)(i) and 162(2)(o)(i) speak to some of those activities. With respect to advisory opinions, in comparison to contentious cases in Article 187, it appears that the jurisdiction of the Chamber is considerably wider in subject-matter. The Chamber's power to provide advisory opinions is set out in a separate provision to Article 187, indicating additional competence enjoyed by the Chamber. The usefulness of the advisory opinion is limited to disputes concerning the legal interpretation of Article 82 and the Authority's powers and functions in that regard. In a scenario where the OCS State violates its obligation, the advisory opinion is of less utility. The relief obtained will consist of a legal opinion which, while giving it legal and moral authority in its dispute, does not enable it to compel the OCS State to comply with its obligation.

A further possibility stems from the competence of ITLOS (not limited to the Chamber) as set out in its own statute in Annex VI.[192] The provisions on competence anticipate the possibility of States Parties and other entities appearing before it, either as provided in Part XI or "in any cases submitted pursuant to any other agreement

---

[187] This hypothetical scenario assumes that a plausible argument to ground the Chamber's jurisdiction to entertain Article 82 disputes can be made.

[188] Ibid., Art. 189. "Its jurisdiction in this regard shall be confined to deciding claims that the application of any rules, regulations and procedures of the ISA in individual cases would be in conflict with the contractual obligations of the parties to the dispute or their obligations under this Convention, claims concerning excess of jurisdiction or misuse of power, and to claims for damages to be paid or other remedy to be given to the party concerned for the failure of the other party to comply with its contractual obligations or its obligations under this Convention."

[189] LOS Convention, supra note 1, Art. 286.

[190] M. H. Nordquist, S. Rosenne and L. B. Sohn, eds., *United Nations Convention on the Law of the Sea 1982: A Commentary*, Vol. V (Dordrecht: Nijhoff, 1989), 36.

[191] ILA Report, supra note 71, section 4.

[192] Chircop, supra note 86, 410-411.

conferring jurisdiction on the Tribunal which is accepted by all the parties."[193] This text is generic enough not to exclude the possibility that "any other agreement" could be a special agreement between an OCS State and the Authority (i.e., the Article 82 Agreement) conferring jurisdiction on the Tribunal. As pointed out by the President of the Tribunal, this is an important procedural innovation brought about by the Convention. Whilst advisory opinions are non-binding, they can play an important role in clarifying the interpretation of the law and thus provide a flexible mechanism for those seeking to clarify particular issues concerning the interpretation or application of the provisions of the Convention.[194]

The second observation made by the ILA Report is the scenario of a State Party (as complainant) deciding to engage Part XV dispute settlement procedures in relation to the OCS State concerning the interpretation or application of the Convention.[195] Without delving into the details or practicalities of Part XV dispute settlement procedures, this plausible scenario calls for additional comments as the Convention anticipates other steps occurring first. There would need to be a dispute between the complainant and OCS States concerning the interpretation of Article 82. Since all States Parties to the LOS Convention are designated as beneficiaries of Article 82, any State Party is in a position to submit a request to the appropriate court or tribunal. Lack of pecuniary prejudice by a complainant will not likely be a bar to a judicial body taking cognizance of the claim.[196] The situation must be one where no settlement is reached by recourse to Section 1 of Part XV, which enables the two States (complainant and OCS States) to resolve the dispute by any peaceful means of their choice.[197] At a minimum, they have an obligation to exchange views regarding settlement by negotiation or other peaceful means.[198] There is also the possibility of resort to conciliation.[199] Ultimately, whilst certain disputes concerning the interpretation or application of the Convention with regard to the exercise by a coastal State of its sovereign rights or jurisdiction, as provided for in the Convention, are excluded from the application of Section 2 of Part XV under article 297, it does not appear that Article 82 disputes are included in the exclusions and optional exceptions to compulsory jurisdiction in Section 2.

---

[193] LOS Convention, supra note 1, Annex VI, Arts. 20(1), 21 and 22. See also Art. 288 in the main text of the Convention, as well as Art. 138 of the Rules of Procedure of the Tribunal.

[194] H. E. Jose Luis Jesus, President of the International Tribunal for the Law of the Sea, Address to the Friends of the Tribunal, New York, 23 June 2009.

[195] LOS Convention, supra note 1, Art. 286.

[196] A potentially useful analogy and authority on this point is the *Case of the S.S. "Wimbledon"* (Britain, France, Italy & Japan (with Poland as Intervener) vs. Germany), P.C.I.J., Ser. A., No. 1, 1923, pp. 5-6, http://www.worldcourts.com/pcij/eng/decisions/1923.08.17_wimbledon/.

[197] Ibid., Art. 280.

[198] Ibid., Art. 283(1).

[199] Ibid., Art. 284 read against Art. 285. Art. 285 extends the application of Part XV, Section 1, to entities other than States Parties. The reference to "party" in Annex V on Conciliation, Art.1, is not restricted to States Parties. Although arbitration under Annex VII does not seem to apply to non-State entities (because Art. 285 does not apply to Part XV, Section 2), in reality Section 1 allows disputants (States and entities) to choose their own dispute settlement procedures. Ibid., Art. 280.

The challenges associated with the resolution of Article 82 disputes highlight the need for close cooperation between the concerned OCS State and the Authority to resolve differences before they degenerate into disputes. Article 285 was negotiated with the spirit and intention to enable States Parties and the Authority to resolve their disputes in accordance with any means of their choice.[200] The ideal Article 82 dispute resolution scenario is one where the OCS State and the Authority consent to the jurisdiction of the Chamber (or the plenary tribunal) by virtue of the Article 82 Agreement, which the Tribunal would take cognizance of under Annex VI of the LOS Convention as a case submitted pursuant to an agreement conferring jurisdiction on the Tribunal and is accepted by the parties concerned.

---

[200] LOS Convention, supra note 1, Art. 280; Nordquist et al., supra note 190, 35-36.

8. CONCLUSION

In the last few decades the international community has gained extensive experience in handling international equity concerns in diplomatic arenas. The political demands of the New International Economic Order have led to numerous in-roads in international law to adjust, if not re-design, the international legal system to better reflect and respond to international inequities.[201]

Article 82 is essentially a provision designed to address international inequity. Clearly, it has ambiguities resulting from its novelty, the difficult compromise behind it and because it is a provision that was negotiated with the knowledge of the 1970s. Its implementation should be guided by fair, reasonable, pragmatic and functional interpretation. Article 82 is a provision that requires international cooperation in its implementation.

While Article 82 remains dormant, it is timely for the International Seabed Authority to consider developing a strategy for the implementation of this provision. In particular, the following steps should be considered for inclusion in the strategy:

- The first step is to introduce the subject to Member States. Article 82 could be brought to the attention of Member States in the Secretary-General's Annual Report through a short explanation of the provision and the practical issues of implementation that it entails.
- Member States should be invited to consider including Article 82 in the Authority's programme of work.
- Upon inclusion in the programme of work, the Legal and Technical Commission should commence consideration of the Authority's implementation responsibilities and eventually to forward to the Council appropriate recommendations for rules, regulations and procedures.
- The Authority needs to start considering developing an arrangement with OCS States as key actors in giving effectivity to Article 82. The development of implementation guidelines to assist the governments of the numerous OCS States potentially affected by Article 82 should be considered.
- The equitable distribution of payments and contributions needs a well-developed framework, process and criteria. The Authority should convene a workshop of experts from Member States to consider practical options for further consideration by the Legal and Technical Commission.
- On the advice of the Legal and Technical Commission, the Council will need to propose to the Assembly the rules, regulations and procedures on equitable sharing of Article 82 benefits.

In addition to the Authority's strategy, it would be useful for ITLOS to anticipate the demands of Article 82 disputes. A seminar involving Tribunal judges could explore how the dispute settlement framework in the LOS Convention might be of assistance to States Parties in resolving such disputes.

---

[201] On the topic of international inequity, see Peter Bautista Payoyo, *Cries of the Sea: World Inequality, Sustainable Development and the Common Heritage of Humanity* (Leiden: Nijhoff, 1997).

ANNEX I

Tasks and Issues for OCS States

Phases	Tasks	Issues
Phase 1 -- pre-production: before and during the granting of prospecting, exploration & development licences, but before commencement of commercial production.	Policy development in support of the domestic implementation of Article 82. Determination of relationship to existing national energy/royalty, international development, GHG reductions, clean development mechanism and other pertinent policies. Consult with sub-national levels of government (if applicable) and minerals, petroleum and other industries concerned with the offshore non-living resources.	How to use the grace period as a period of transition. Whether payments and contributions will be absorbed by national authorities or not: (1) if yes, will the national government absorb the fiscal cost for defined periods or permanently? (2) if not or if absorbed for defined periods, at what other level will they be absorbed? (3) where producers are to absorb the cost, when would the levy of the OCS royalty commence? Would "contingent" royalty levies be necessary? Would any pre-existing production licences need to be grandfathered? (4) alternatively, the State might share the fiscal responsibility with a sub-national level of government or the licenced producer, or both.
	Development of the legal framework or amendment of existing domestic licensing regime to implement Article 82.	Depending on the domestic level at which the payments and contribution will be absorbed: (1) if sub-national levels of government are involved, what political and legal arrangement is appropriate? (2) if industry producers are involved, what changes will be needed to the existing royalty regime? Will they apply to existing and/or future production licences?

Phases	Tasks	Issues
	Enhancing the mandates of national authorities responsible for the allocation, administration and monitoring of production licences and receipt of royalty revenues. Development of the necessary management and administrative framework to collect and process payments and contributions. Notice 1: Providing notice to the ISA of exploration licensing on the OCS.	How to levy and administer the rising scale of payments or contributions in coordination with or as part of the domestic royalty regime(s). In cases where royalty holidays/relief or related fiscal incentives are available to producers, how would the levy of the OCS royalty apply? Determining the administrative cost of the levy and where the cost will lie (Article 82 does not appear to permit deductions).
Phase 2 -- grace period: between commencement of production and until the end of the 5th year of production.	Notice 2: Provide the ISA with notice of the prospective application of the obligation in its regard, and including: Official date of commencement of commercial production. Type of non-living resource. Site (location of the resource): whether the resource is located within the OCS of the OCS State in its entirety, or straddles (a) its EEZ, or (b) the OCS or EEZ of a neighbouring State, or (c) the Area.	How much and what type of information to be provided in the notice to the ISA. Timing of notices to the ISA.

Phases	Tasks	Issues
	Anticipate whether the State obligation will be discharged through payments or contributions in kind. Payments: determine the currency of payment with reference to the ISA's Article 82 Rules & Regulations (to be developed). Contributions in kind in consultation with the ISA's Article 82 Rules & Regulations (to be developed) and in consultation with the ISA. Decide on how and when payments or contributions will be made (including decision on calendar or fiscal year or period).	Determining how payments will be calculated and determining the nature of the in-kind contributions and their delivery.
	Anticipation of the impact of the levy in relation to existing contracting practices (e.g., concessions, production-sharing, service agreements, etc.).	
	Development of an appropriate collection & accounting procedure and practice.	
	Notice 3: Provide the ISA with notice of the decision on whether the obligation will be discharged through payments or contributions in kind.	
	Enter into an Article 82 Agreement with the ISA.	

Phases	Tasks	Issues
Phase 3 -- OCS royalty: payment period commencing with the 6th year of production.	Determination of actual total production for the first and subsequent years (including deducting amounts of the resource in question used in connection with production).	How much technical, economic and management information the ISA needs to be able to discharge its responsibilities in Article 82, and any proprietary and confidentiality matters relating to sensitive commercial information.
	Ongoing determination of the value and volume of payments or contributions, as appropriate.	Determining the well-head value or volume of payments and contributions in kind (if a share of the resource) and the delivery of contributions in kind. Factoring in periods of suspension of production.
	Notification to the ISA of unexpected changes or interruptions to total production which are likely to affect the amount of payments or contributions.	

ANNEX II

Tasks and Issues for the Authority

Phases	Tasks	Issues
(1) Pre-production Phase: period before commencement of OCS commercial production.	Determining the full extent of the ISA's mandate and the consequent powers and functions and whether any aspects of the implementation of Article 82 might require the endorsement of the ISA Membership or SPLOS endorsement.	Producing an acceptable interpretation of explicit and implicit powers and functions in relation to Article 82. Clarifying the scope of the Council's powers and functions to make rules, regulations and procedures in Article 160(2)(o)(i). Determining the Council's authority to take action to secure compliance with its rules, regulations and procedures in Article 160(2)(o)(i). Clarify role and tasks of the Legal and Technical Commission. Whether ISA Membership and/or SPLOS endorsement of the ISA's interpretation of its mandate is needed. Whether an advisory opinion from ITLOS is needed.
	Development of policy directions for Article 82 implementation. Determine whether SPLOS endorsement is needed. Consideration and adoption by Council and Assembly.	Identifying appropriate goals for the distribution of payments and contributions (e.g., to assist adaptation to climate change related response and mitigation strategies, assist integrated coastal and ocean management, etc.). Determining the extent to which policies, rules & procedures/processes developed or that will be developed for activities in the Area can be transposed to the ISA's responsibilities in Article 82 (e.g., currency matters, equitable criteria for distribution of benefits, etc.).

Phases	Tasks	Issues
	Development of an administrative structure to receive payments and contributions in kind.	Determining the extent of its overseeing functions in relation to payments and in-kind contributions received.
	Anticipation of the administrative needs of contributions in kind.	Determining and covering the costs of administering the receipt and distribution of payments or contributions.
	Development of rules, regulations and procedures.	Determining the institutional (including personnel) capacity-building needed in the ISA.
	Development of a monitoring, accounting and auditing system for incoming payments and contributions.	Determining its knowledge needs of the extent and nature of production that will form the basis of a particular OCS State's payment or contributions (e.g., resource and site specific technical matters, calculations concerning all production, value, etc.).
		Determining the extent to which, if at all, the ISA can monitor and audit payments and contributions in kind.
	Anticipation of OCS States likely to be first engaged by Article 82.	
	Identifying national authority contact points in OCS States.	
	Development of guidelines for the domestic implementation of Article 82 in consultation with interested OCS and other States.	
	Monitoring activities on OCSs around the world that might become Article 82 eligible.	

Phases	Tasks	Issues
(2) Grace Period Phase: period between com- mencement of production and until the end of the 5th year of production.	Acknowledgement of receipt of Notices from an OCS State concerning activities on the OCS and the prospective application of the obligation in its regard.	
	Development of equitable criteria for eligibility and distribution of the payments and contributions. Development of rules, regulations and procedures. Development of an appropriate composite index for the ranking of beneficiaries. Determination of the procedure for the distribution of benefits and related safeguards. Deciding on whether to administer benefits internally (establish a trust fund, e.g., Common Heritage Fund) or delegate distribution existing mechanisms.	Determining equitable criteria and developing a composite index that appropriately reflects those criteria. Ranking States/peoples: applying and reviewing the composite index listing beneficiary States/peoples. Developing additional capacity to administer the trust fund, if this is opted for. If there is delegation to existing mechanisms, need to determine what mechanisms to use and to enter into agreements with pertinent institutions.
	Development of Model Article 82 Agreement(s) for receiving payments and contributions. Consult OCS States and involve experts from those and other States to develop standard terms of model agreement. Identify the acceptable currency(ies) for payments.	Securing the cooperation of key OCS States. Formulating an appropriate dispute settlement procedure for Article 82 disputes.

	Identify potential arrangements for managing in-kind contributions and related costs as guideline for OCS States and the ISA.	
	Acknowledgement of receipt of notice concerning the OCS State's decision on the obligation to be discharged through payments or contributions in kind.	
	Enter into an Article 82 Agreement with the producing OCS State.	
(3) OCS Royalty Phase: period commencing with the 6th year of production.	Developing and maintaining a working relationship with OCS States and their designated counterpart authorities, and other beneficiary States.	
	Receiving payments and contributions in kind.	Managing fluctuating values of payments and contributions in kind as a result of fluctuations in currency values and commodity prices.
	Ongoing review of equitable criteria and ranking of beneficiaries for the distribution of benefits.	
	Distribution of benefits.	Administering the distribution of benefits in an equitable manner.

ANNEX III
Relevant Provisions of the LOS Convention

PART VI
CONTINENTAL SHELF

Article 76
Definition of the continental shelf

1.   The continental shelf of a coastal State comprises the seabed and subsoil of the submarine areas that extend beyond its territorial sea throughout the natural prolongation of its land territory to the outer edge of the continental margin, or to a distance of 200 nautical miles from the baselines from which the breadth of the territorial sea is measured where the outer edge of the continental margin does not extend up to that distance.

2.   The continental shelf of a coastal State shall not extend beyond the limits provided for in paragraphs 4 to 6.

3.   The continental margin comprises the submerged prolongation of the land mass of the coastal State, and consists of the seabed and subsoil of the shelf, the slope and the rise. It does not include the deep ocean floor with its oceanic ridges or the subsoil thereof.

4.   (a) For the purposes of this Convention, the coastal State shall establish the outer edge of the continental margin wherever the margin extends beyond 200 nautical miles from the baselines from which the breadth of the territorial sea is measured, by either:

> (i)   a line delineated in accordance with paragraph 7 by reference to the outermost fixed points at each of which the thickness of sedimentary rocks is at least 1 per cent of the shortest distance from such point to the foot of the continental slope; or
>
> (ii)   a line delineated in accordance with paragraph 7 by reference to fixed points not more than 60 nautical miles from the foot of the continental slope.

(b)   In the absence of evidence to the contrary, the foot of the continental slope shall be determined as the point of maximum change in the gradient at its base.

5.   The fixed points comprising the line of the outer limits of the continental shelf on the seabed, drawn in accordance with paragraph 4 (a)(i) and (ii), either shall not exceed 350 nautical miles from the baselines from which the breadth of the territorial sea is measured or shall not exceed 100 nautical miles from the 2,500 metre isobath, which is a line connecting the depth of 2,500 metres.

6.   Notwithstanding the provisions of paragraph 5, on submarine ridges, the outer limit of the continental shelf shall not exceed 350 nautical miles from the baselines from which the breadth of the territorial sea is measured. This paragraph does not apply to submarine elevations that are natural components of the continental margin, such as its plateaux, rises, caps, banks and spurs.

7.   The coastal State shall delineate the outer limits of its continental shelf, where that shelf extends beyond 200 nautical miles from the baselines from which the breadth of the territorial sea is measured, by straight lines not exceeding 60 nautical miles in length, connecting fixed points, defined by coordinates of latitude and longitude.

8.   Information on the limits of the continental shelf beyond 200 nautical miles from the baselines from which the breadth of the territorial sea is measured shall be submitted by the coastal State to the Commission on the Limits of the Continental Shelf set up under Annex II on the basis of equitable geographical representation. The Commission shall make recommendations to coastal States on matters related to the establishment of the outer limits of their continental shelf. The limits of the shelf established by a coastal State on the basis of these recommendations shall be final and binding.

9.   The coastal State shall deposit with the Secretary-General of the United Nations charts and relevant information, including geodetic data, permanently describing the outer limits of its continental shelf. The Secretary-General shall give due publicity thereto.

10.   The provisions of this article are without prejudice to the question of delimitation of the continental shelf between States with opposite or adjacent coasts.

Article 77
Rights of the coastal State over the continental shelf

1.   The coastal State exercises over the continental shelf sovereign rights for the purpose of exploring it and exploiting its natural resources.

2.   The rights referred to in paragraph 1 are exclusive in the sense that if the coastal State does not explore the continental shelf or exploit its natural resources, no one may undertake these activities without the express consent of the coastal State.

3.   The rights of the coastal State over the continental shelf do not depend on occupation, effective or notional, or on any express proclamation.

4.   The natural resources referred to in this Part consist of the mineral and other non-living resources of the seabed and subsoil together with living organisms belonging to sedentary species, that is to say, organisms which, at the harvestable stage, either are immobile on or under the seabed or are unable to move except in constant physical contact with the seabed or the subsoil.

Article 82
Payments and contributions with respect to the exploitation of the continental shelf beyond 200 nautical miles

1.   The coastal State shall make payments or contributions in kind in respect of the exploitation of the non-living resources of the continental shelf beyond 200 nautical miles from the baselines from which the breadth of the territorial sea is measured.

2.   The payments and contributions shall be made annually with respect to all production at a site after the first five years of production at that site. For the sixth year, the rate of payment or contribution shall be 1 per cent of the value or volume of production at the site. The rate shall increase by 1 per cent for each subsequent year

until the twelfth year and shall remain at 7 per cent thereafter. Production does not include resources used in connection with exploitation.

3. A developing State which is a net importer of a mineral resource produced from its continental shelf is exempt from making such payments or contributions in respect of that mineral resource.

4. The payments or contributions shall be made through the Authority, which shall distribute them to States Parties to this Convention, on the basis of equitable sharing criteria, taking into account the interests and needs of developing States, particularly the least developed and the land-locked among them.

PART XI: THE AREA
SECTION 1. GENERAL PROVISIONS

Article 133
Use of terms

For the purposes of this Part:

(a) "resources" means all solid, liquid or gaseous mineral resources *in situ* in the Area at or beneath the seabed, including polymetallic nodules;

(b) resources, when recovered from the Area, are referred to as "minerals".

Article 134
Scope of this Part

1. This Part applies to the Area.
2. Activities in the Area shall be governed by the provisions of this Part.
3. The requirements concerning deposit of, and publicity to be given to, the charts or lists of geographical coordinates showing the limits referred to in article 1, paragraph l(1), are set forth in Part VI.
4. Nothing in this article affects the establishment of the outer limits of the continental shelf in accordance with Part VI or the validity of agreements relating to delimitation between States with opposite or adjacent coasts.

SECTION 2. PRINCIPLES GOVERNING THE AREA

Article 136
Common heritage of mankind

The Area and its resources are the common heritage of mankind.

Article 137
Legal status of the Area and its resources

1. No State shall claim or exercise sovereignty or sovereign rights over any part of the Area or its resources, nor shall any State or natural or juridical person appropriate

any part thereof. No such claim or exercise of sovereignty or sovereign rights nor such appropriation shall be recognized.

2.   All rights in the resources of the Area are vested in mankind as a whole, on whose behalf the Authority shall act. These resources are not subject to alienation. The minerals recovered from the Area, however, may only be alienated in accordance with this Part and the rules, regulations and procedures of the Authority.

3.   No State or natural or juridical person shall claim, acquire or exercise rights with respect to the minerals recovered from the Area except in accordance with this Part. Otherwise, no such claim, acquisition or exercise of such rights shall be recognized.

Article 140
Benefit of mankind

1.   Activities in the Area shall, as specifically provided for in this Part, be carried out for the benefit of mankind as a whole, irrespective of the geographical location of States, whether coastal or land-locked, and taking into particular consideration the interests and needs of developing States and of peoples who have not attained full independence or other self-governing status recognized by the United Nations in accordance with General Assembly resolution 1514 (XV) and other relevant General Assembly resolutions.

2.   The Authority shall provide for the equitable sharing of financial and other economic benefits derived from activities in the Area through any appropriate mechanism, on a non-discriminatory basis, in accordance with article 160, paragraph 2(f)(i).

Article 142
Rights and legitimate interests of coastal States

1.   Activities in the Area, with respect to resource deposits in the Area which lie across limits of national jurisdiction, shall be conducted with due regard to the rights and legitimate interests of any coastal State across whose jurisdiction such deposits lie.

2.   Consultations, including a system of prior notification, shall be maintained with the State concerned, with a view to avoiding infringement of such rights and interests. In cases where activities in the Area may result in the exploitation of resources lying within national jurisdiction, the prior consent of the coastal State concerned shall be required.

3.   Neither this Part nor any rights granted or exercised pursuant thereto shall affect the rights of coastal States to take such measures consistent with the relevant provisions of Part XII as may be necessary to prevent, mitigate or eliminate grave and imminent danger to their coastline, or related interests from pollution or threat thereof or from other hazardous occurrences resulting from or caused by any activities in the Area.

Article 148
Participation of developing States in activities in the Area

The effective participation of developing States in activities in the Area shall be promoted as specifically provided for in this Part, having due regard to their special interests and needs, and in particular to the special need of the land-locked and geographically disadvantaged among them to overcome obstacles arising from their disadvantaged location, including remoteness from the Area and difficulty of access to and from it.

SECTION 4. THE AUTHORITY
SUBSECTION A. GENERAL PROVISIONS

Article156
Establishment of the Authority

1.   There is hereby established the International Seabed Authority, which shall function in accordance with this Part.

2.   All States Parties are *ipso facto* members of the Authority.

3.   Observers at the Third United Nations Conference on the Law of the Sea who have signed the Final Act and who are not referred to in article 305, paragraph 1(c), (d), (e) or (f), shall have the right to participate in the Authority as observers, in accordance with its rules, regulations and procedures.

4.   The seat of the Authority shall be in Jamaica.

5.   The Authority may establish such regional centres or offices as it deems necessary for the exercise of its functions.

Article 157
Nature and fundamental principles of the Authority

1.   The Authority is the organization through which States Parties shall, in accordance with this Part, organize and control activities in the Area, particularly with a view to administering the resources of the Area.

2.   The powers and functions of the Authority shall be those expressly conferred upon it by this Convention. The Authority shall have such incidental powers, consistent with this Convention, as are implicit in and necessary for the exercise of those powers and functions with respect to activities in the Area.

3.   The Authority is based on the principle of the sovereign equality of all its members.

4.   All members of the Authority shall fulfil in good faith the obligations assumed by them in accordance with this Part in order to ensure to all of them the rights and benefits resulting from membership.

Article 158
Organs of the Authority

1.   There are hereby established, as the principal organs of the Authority, an Assembly, a Council and a Secretariat.

2.   There is hereby established the Enterprise, the organ through which the Authority shall carry out the functions referred to in article 170, paragraph 1.

3.   Such subsidiary organs as may be found necessary may be established in accordance with this Part.

4.   Each principal organ of the Authority and the Enterprise shall be responsible for exercising those powers and functions which are conferred upon it. In exercising such powers and functions each organ shall avoid taking any action which may derogate from or impede the exercise of specific powers and functions conferred upon another organ.

Article160
Powers and functions

1.   The Assembly, as the sole organ of the Authority consisting of all the members, shall be considered the supreme organ of the Authority to which the other principal organs shall be accountable as specifically provided for in this Convention. The Assembly shall have the power to establish general policies in conformity with the relevant provisions of this Convention on any question or matter within the competence of the Authority.

2.   In addition, the powers and functions of the Assembly shall be:

(f) (i)   to consider and approve, upon the recommendation of the Council, the rules, regulations and procedures on the equitable sharing of financial and other economic benefits derived from activities in the Area and the payments and contributions made pursuant to article 82, taking into particular consideration the interests and needs of developing States and peoples who have not attained full independence or other self-governing status. If the Assembly does not approve the recommendations of the Council, the Assembly shall return them to the Council for reconsideration in the light of the views expressed by the Assembly;

...

Article161
Composition, procedure and voting

...

8. ...

(d) Decisions on questions of substance arising under the following provisions shall be taken by consensus: article 162, paragraph 2(m) and (o); adoption of amendments to Part XI.

...

Article162
Powers and functions

1.   The Council is the executive organ of the Authority. The Council shall have the power to establish, in conformity with this Convention and the general policies established by the Assembly, the specific policies to be pursued by the Authority on any question or matter within the competence of the Authority.

2.   In addition, the Council shall:

...

(o) (i) recommend to the Assembly rules, regulations and procedures on the equitable sharing of financial and other economic benefits derived from activities in the Area and the payments and contributions made pursuant to article 82, taking into particular consideration the interests and needs of the developing States and peoples who have not attained full independence or other self-governing status;

...

Article 163
Organs of the Council

1.   There are hereby established the following organs of the Council:
(a) an Economic Planning Commission;
(b) a Legal and Technical Commission.

...

Article 164
The Economic Planning Commission

1.   Members of the Economic Planning Commission shall have appropriate qualifications such as those relevant to mining, management of mineral resource activities, international trade or international economics. The Council shall endeavour to ensure that the membership of the Commission reflects all appropriate qualifications. The Commission shall include at least two members from developing States whose exports of the categories of minerals to be derived from the Area have a substantial bearing upon their economies.

...

Article 165
The Legal and Technical Commission

1.   Members of the Legal and Technical Commission shall have appropriate qualifications such as those relevant to exploration for and exploitation and processing of mineral resources, oceanology, protection of the marine environment, or economic or legal matters relating to ocean mining and related fields of expertise. The Council shall endeavour to ensure that the membership of the Commission reflects all appropriate qualifications.
2.   The Commission shall:
(a) make recommendations with regard to the exercise of the Authority's functions upon the request of the Council;

...

(f) formulate and submit to the Council the rules, regulations and procedures referred to in article 162, paragraph 2(o), taking into account all relevant factors including assessments of the environmental implications of activities in the Area;

(g) keep such rules, regulations and procedures under review and recommend to the Council from time to time such amendments thereto as it may deem necessary or desirable;

...

(i) recommend to the Council that proceedings be instituted on behalf of the Authority before the Seabed Disputes Chamber, in accordance with this Part and the relevant Annexes taking into account particularly article 187;

(j) make recommendations to the Council with respect to measures to be taken, upon a decision by the Seabed Disputes Chamber in proceedings instituted in accordance with subparagraph (i);

...

Article 171
Funds of the Authority

The funds of the Authority shall include:

(a) assessed contributions made by members of the Authority in accordance with article 160, paragraph 2(e);
(b) funds received by the Authority pursuant to Annex III, article 13, in connection with activities in the Area;
(c) funds transferred from the Enterprise in accordance with Annex IV, article 10;
(d) funds borrowed pursuant to article 174;
(e) voluntary contributions made by members or other entities; and
(f) payments to a compensation fund, in accordance with article 151, paragraph 10, whose sources are to be recommended by the Economic Planning Commission.

Article 172
Annual budget of the Authority

The Secretary-General shall draft the proposed annual budget of the Authority and submit it to the Council. The Council shall consider the proposed annual budget and submit it to the Assembly, together with any recommendations thereon. The Assembly shall consider and approve the proposed annual budget in accordance with article 160, paragraph 2(h).

Article 173
Expenses of the Authority

1. The contributions referred to in article 171, subparagraph (a), shall be paid into a special account to meet the administrative expenses of the Authority until the Authority has sufficient funds from other sources to meet those expenses.

2.   The administrative expenses of the Authority shall be a first call upon the funds of the Authority.

...

Article 176
Legal status

The Authority shall have international legal personality and such legal capacity as may be necessary for the exercise of its functions and the fulfilment of its purposes.

SECTION 5. SETTLEMENT OF DISPUTES AND ADVISORY OPINIONS

Article 186
Seabed Disputes Chamber of the International Tribunal for the Law of the Sea

The establishment of the Seabed Disputes Chamber and the manner in which it shall exercise its jurisdiction shall be governed by the provisions of this section, of Part XV and of Annex VI.

Article 187
Jurisdiction of the Seabed Disputes Chamber

The Seabed Disputes Chamber shall have jurisdiction under this Part and the Annexes relating thereto in disputes with respect to activities in the Area falling within the following categories:

(a)   disputes between States Parties concerning the interpretation or application of this Part and the Annexes relating thereto;

(b)   disputes between a State Party and the Authority concerning:

    (i)   acts or omissions of the Authority or of a State Party alleged to be in violation of this Part or the Annexes relating thereto or of rules, regulations and procedures of the Authority adopted in accordance therewith; or

    (ii)   acts of the Authority alleged to be in excess of jurisdiction or a misuse of power;

...

(f)   any other disputes for which the jurisdiction of the Chamber is specifically provided in this Convention.

...

Article 189
Limitation on jurisdiction with regard to decisions of the Authority

The Seabed Disputes Chamber shall have no jurisdiction with regard to the exercise by the Authority of its discretionary powers in accordance with this Part; in no case shall it substitute its discretion for that of the Authority. Without prejudice to article 191, in exercising its jurisdiction pursuant to article 187, the Seabed Disputes Chamber shall not pronounce itself on the question of whether any rules, regulations and procedures of the Authority are in conformity with this Convention, nor declare invalid any such rules, regulations and procedures. Its jurisdiction in this regard shall be confined to deciding claims that the application of any rules, regulations and procedures of the Authority in individual cases would be in conflict with the contractual obligations of the parties to the dispute or their obligations under this Convention, claims concerning excess of jurisdiction or misuse of power, and to claims for damages to be paid or other remedy to be given to the party concerned for the failure of the other party to comply with its contractual obligations or its obligations under this Convention.

...

Article 191
Advisory opinions

The Seabed Disputes Chamber shall give advisory opinions at the request of the Assembly or the Council on legal questions arising within the scope of their activities. Such opinions shall be given as a matter of urgency.

PART XV
SETTLEMENT OF DISPUTES

SECTION 1. GENERAL PROVISIONS

Article 285
Application of this section to disputes submitted pursuant to Part XI

This section applies to any dispute which pursuant to Part XI, section 5, is to be settled in accordance with procedures provided for in this Part. If an entity other than a State Party is a party to such a dispute, this section applies *mutatis mutandis.*

SECTION 2. COMPULSORY PROCEDURES ENTAILING
BINDING DECISIONS

Article 286
Application of procedures under this section

Subject to section 3, any dispute concerning the interpretation or application of this Convention shall, where no settlement has been reached by recourse to section 1, be submitted at the request of any party to the dispute to the court or tribunal having jurisdiction under this section.

...

Article 288
Jurisdiction

1. A court or tribunal referred to in article 287 shall have jurisdiction over any dispute concerning the interpretation or application of this Convention which is submitted to it in accordance with this Part.

2. A court or tribunal referred to in article 287 shall also have jurisdiction over any dispute concerning the interpretation or application of an international agreement related to the purposes of this Convention, which is submitted to it in accordance with the agreement.

3. The Seabed Disputes Chamber of the International Tribunal for the Law of the Sea established in accordance with Annex VI, and any other chamber or arbitral tribunal referred to in Part XI, section 5, shall have jurisdiction in any matter which is submitted to it in accordance therewith.

4. In the event of a dispute as to whether a court or tribunal has jurisdiction, the matter shall be settled by decision of that court or tribunal.

    …

Article 291
Access

1. All the dispute settlement procedures specified in this Part shall be open to States Parties.

2. The dispute settlement procedures specified in this Part shall be open to entities other than States Parties only as specifically provided for in this Convention.

PART XVI
GENERAL PROVISIONS

Article 300
Good faith and abuse of rights

States Parties shall fulfil in good faith the obligations assumed under this Convention and shall exercise the rights, jurisdiction and freedoms recognized in this Convention in a manner which would not constitute an abuse of right.

PART XVII
FINAL PROVISIONS

Article 309
Reservations and exceptions

No reservations or exceptions may be made to this Convention unless expressly permitted by other articles of this Convention.

Article 311
Relation to other conventions and international agreements

1.   This Convention shall prevail, as between States Parties, over the Geneva Conventions on the Law of the Sea of 29 April 1958.

...

Article 317
Denunciation

1.   A State Party may, by written notification addressed to the Secretary-General of the United Nations, denounce this Convention and may indicate its reasons. Failure to indicate reasons shall not affect the validity of the denunciation. The denunciation shall take effect one year after the date of receipt of the notification, unless the notification specifies a later date.

2.   A State shall not be discharged by reason of the denunciation from the financial and contractual obligations which accrued while it was a Party to this Convention, nor shall the denunciation affect any right, obligation or legal situation of that State created through the execution of this Convention prior to its termination for that State.

3.   The denunciation shall not in any way affect the duty of any State Party to fulfil any obligation embodied in this Convention to which it would be subject under international law independently of this Convention.

Article 320
Authentic texts

The original of this Convention, of which the Arabic, Chinese, English, French, Russian and Spanish texts are equally authentic, shall, subject to article 305, paragraph 2, be deposited with the Secretary-General of the United Nations.

ANNEX IV

LIST OF PARTICIPANTS
AT THE SEMINAR ON ISSUES ASSOCIATED WITH
THE IMPLEMENTATION OF ARTICLE 82 OF
THE UNITED NATIONS CONVENTION ON THE LAW OF THE SEA

Chatham House, London
11 – 13 February 2009

Invited Participants

Mr David Anderson
7 Onslow Crescent
Chislehurst
Kent, BR7 5RW
United Kingdom

D.H.Anderson@btinternet.com

Mr J.P. Andrews
Canada-Newfoundland and Labrador Offshore
  Petroleum Board
5th Floor, TD Place
140 Water Street
St. John's, NL
Canada A1C 6H6

jandrews@cnlopb.nl.ca

Mr Paul Barnes
Manager – Atlantic Canada
Canadian Association of Petroleum Producers
403, 235 Water Street
St. John's, NL
Canada, A1C 1BC

barnes@capp.ca

Professor Arne Bjorlykke
Geological Survey of Norway
NO-7491 Trondheim
Norway

arne.bjorlykke@ngu.no

Mr Gritakumar E. Chitty
14/1 Cambridge Place
Colombo 7
Sri Lanka

gechitty@gmail.com

Mr Tim Daniel
Edwards, Angell, Palmer & Dodge
1 Fetter Lane
London, EC4A 1JB

TDaniel@eapdlaw.com

Ambassador Hasjim Djalal
Jalan Kemang IV, No. 10A
Jakarta Selatan
Indonesia

hdh@cbn.net.id

Dr David Freestone
Lobingier Visiting Professor of Comparative
  Law and Jurisprudence
The George Washington University Law School
2000 H St NW
Washington DC 20052

dfreestone@law.gwu.edu

Dr Kaiser Gonçalves de Souza
Chief, Division of Marine Geology
Geological Survey of Brazil (CPRM)
Ministry of Mines and Energy
Headquarters: SGAN 603
Conj. J, Parte A, 1st floor
70.830-030 – Brasília – DF

Kaisers@df.cprm.gov.br

Prof. Dr Gao Zhiguo
Director General
China Institute of Marine Affairs
State Oceanic Administration
1 Fuxingmenwai Avenue
Beijing 100860
The People's Republic of China

zgao@cima.gov.cn

Mr Huang Baoguang
Consulting Manager, Legal Department
China National Offshore Oil Corporation
P.O. Box 4705
No. 25 Chao Yang Men North Street
Dongcheng District
Beijing 100010
The People's Republic of China

huangbg@cnooc.com.cn

Mr Paul L. Kelly
Energy & Ocean Policy Consultant
5555 Del Monte Drive, Suite T-23
Houston, Texas 77056
U.S.A

paullkelly@aol.com

Professor Keyuan Zou
Harris Professor of International Law
Lancashire Law School
University of Central Lancashire
Preston, United Kingdom PR1 2HE

KZou@uclan.ac.uk

Professor Ted L. McDorman
University of Victoria
Faculty of Law
PO Box 2400 STN CSC
Victoria, British Columbia
Canada   V8W 3H7

tlmcdorm@uvic.ca

Ambassador Satya N. Nandan
New York
U.S.A.

Satya.n.nandan@gmail.com

Judge Dolliver Nelson
International Tribunal for the Law of the Sea
Hamburg, Germany

dnelson@btinternet.com

Mr David Ong
Reader in International & Environmental Law
University of Essex Law School
Wivenhoe Park, Colchester
Essex CO4 3SQ

daveo@essex.ac.uk

Dr Frida Armas Pfirter
Paraguay 1545
1061-Buenos Aires
Argentina

Frida_Armas@yahoo.com

Mr Mahmoud Ahmed Samir Samy
Minister Plenipotentiary
Deputy Assistant Minister of Foreign Affairs
Cairo, Egypt

mssamy@hotmail.com

Mr Walter De Sá Leitão
Av. Chile 65 ala 701 Centro
Rio de Janeiro
Brazil

saleitao@petrobras.com.br

Dr Rashid Sumaila
Fisheries Economics Research Unit
Fisheries Centre
University of British Columbia
2202 Main Mall,
Vancouver, B.C., V6T
Canada

r.sumaila@fisheries.ubc.ca

Professor Dr Rüdiger Wolfrum
Max Planck Institute for Comparative Public
    Law and International Law
Im Neuenheimer Feld 535
69120 Heidelberg
Germany

wolfrum@mpil.de

Dr Ibibia Lucky Worika
General Legal Counsel
Organization of Petroleum Exporting Countries
    (OPEC)
Obere Donaustrasse 93
A-1020 Vienna,
Austria

ilworika@opec.org

Resource personnel

Dr Lindsay Parson
National Oceanography Centre
University of Southampton
Waterfront Campus, European Way
Southampton SO14 3ZH
United Kingdom

L.Parson@noc.soton.ac.uk

Dr Aldo Chircop
Professor of Law
Marine & Environmental Law Institute
Dalhousie University
Halifax, NS, B3H 4H9
Canada

Aldo.Chircop@Dal.Ca

International Seabed Authority

Nii Allotey Odunton
Secretary-General

nodunton@isa.org.jm

Michael Lodge
Legal Adviser

mlodge@isa.org.jm

Kening Zhang
Senior Legal Officer

kzhang@isa.org.jm

Chatham House

Bernice Lee
Head, Energy, Environment and Development
Programme

blee@chathamhouse.org

Duncan Brack
Senior Research Fellow

dbrack@chathamhouse.org

Heike Baumüller
Senior Research Fellow

Cleo Paskal
Associate Fellow

me@cleopaskal.com

LITERATURE CITED

1. PRIMARY MATERIALS

1.1 International instruments

Agenda 21, The Programme of Action from Rio, adopted at the United Nations Conference on Environment and Development, Rio de Janeiro, 3-14 June 1992, http://www.un.org/esa/sustdev/documents/agenda21/english/agenda21toc.htm.

Statute of the International Court of Justice, 39 *A.J.I.L. Supp.* 215 (1945), http://www.icj-cij.org/icjwww/ibasicdocuments/ibasictext/ibasicstatute.htm#CHAPTER_II.

Convention on the Continental Shelf, Geneva, 29 April 1958, 499 *U.N.T.S.* 312-321.

Convention on the Law of Treaties, Vienna, 23 May 1969, 1155 *U.N.T.S.* 331.

Vienna Convention on the Law of Treaties between States and International Organizations or between International Organizations, Vienna, 21 March 1986, United Nations Treaty Collection, http://untreaty.un.org/ilc/texts/instruments/english/conventions/1_2_1986.pdf.

Global Programme of Action for the Protection of the Marine Environment from Land-Based Activities, adopted at the Intergovernmental Conference to adopt a Global Programme of Action for the Protection of the Marine Environment from Land-Based Activities, Washington, 23 October-3 November 1995, UN Doc. UNEP(OCA)/LBA/IG.2/7, 5 December 1995, http://www.gpa.unep.org/documents/full_text_of_the_english.pdf.

International Convention on the Establishment of an International Fund for Compensation for Oil Pollution Damage, London, 18 December 1971, 1110 *U.N.T.S.* 57.

————— *Protocol to Amend the International Convention on the Establishment of an International Fund for Compensation for Oil Pollution Damage, 1971*, London, 27 November 1992, 1996 A.T.S. 3.

————— *Protocol of 2003 to the International Convention on the Establishment of an International Fund for Compensation for Oil Pollution Damage, 1992*, London, 16 May 2003, IMO Doc. LEG/CONF.14/20.

————— *International Oil Pollution Compensation Funds*: Consolidated versions, http://www.iopcfund.org/.

United Nations Convention on the Law of the Sea, Montego Bay, 10 December 1982, 1833 *U.N.T.S.* 3.

————— *The Law of the Sea: Compendium of Basic Documents:* Consolidated version (Kingston, Jamaica: International Seabed Authority and Caribbean Law Publishing Co., 2001), 1-205.

Final Act of the Third United Nations Conference on the Law of the Sea, Montego Bay, 10 December 1982, http://www.un.org/Depts/los/convention_agreements/texts/final_act_eng.pdf.

The Law of the Sea: Compendium of Basic Documents (Kingston, Jamaica: International Seabed Authority and Caribbean Law Publishing Co., 2001).

United Nations Framework Convention on Climate Change, New York, 9 May 1992, http://unfccc.int/resource/docs/convkp/conveng.pdf.

————— *Kyoto Protocol to the United Nations Framework Convention on Climate Change*, Kyoto, 11 December 1997, http://unfccc.int/resource/docs/convkp/kpeng.pdf.

Agreement relating to the Implementation of Part XI of the United Nations Convention on the Law of the Sea of 10 December 1982, New York, 28 July 1994, UN Doc. A/RES/48/263, 17 August 1994, http://daccessdds.un.org/doc/UNDOC/GEN/N94/332/98/PDF/N9433298.pdf?OpenElement.

――――――― *The Law of the Sea: Compendium of Basic Documents:* Consolidated version (Kingston, Jamaica: International Seabed Authority and Caribbean Law Publishing Co., 2001), 208-225.

Agreement for the Implementation of the Provisions of the United Nations Convention on the Law of the Sea of 10 December 1982 relating to the Conservation and Management of Straddling Fish Stocks and Highly Migratory Fish Stocks, New York, 4 December 1995. *The Law of the Sea: Compendium of Basic Documents* (Kingston, Jamaica: International Seabed Authority and Caribbean Law Publishing Co., 2001), 271-305.

United Nations Millennium Declaration, United Nations General Assembly Resolution 55/2, UN Doc. A/RES/55/2, 18 September 2000, http://www.un.org/millennium/declaration/ares552e.htm.

1.2 Cases

Suriname/Guyana, Permanent Court of Arbitration (Award), 17 September 2007, http://www.pca-cpa.org/showpage.asp?pag_id=1147.

Case of the S.S. "Wimbledon" (Britain, France, Italy & Japan (with Poland as Intervener) vs. Germany), P.C.I.J., Ser. A., No. 1, 1923. http://www.worldcourts.com/pcij/eng/decisions/1923.08.17_wimbledon/.

1.3 Conference records and documentary compilations

International Seabed Authority: Basic Texts (Kingston, Jamaica: International Seabed Authority, 2003).

International Seabed Authority, Assembly, Ninth Session (Report), Kingston, Jamaica, 28 July-8 August 2002, ISBA/9/A/9, 7 August 2003.

International Seabed Authority, *The Law of the Sea: Compendium of Basic Documents* (Kingston, Jamaica: International Seabed Authority and Caribbean Law Publishing Co., 2001).

Platzöder, Renate, ed., *Third United Nations Conference on the Law of the Sea: Documents,* Vols. I-XVIII (Dobbs Ferry, N.Y.: Oceana Publications, 1982-1988).

Report of the International Conference on Financing for Development, Monterrey (Monterrey Consensus), Mexico, 18-22 March 2002, UN Doc. A/CONF.198/11 (New York: United Nations, 2002), http://www.unmillenniumproject.org/documents/07_aconf198-11.pdf.

United Nations Conference on the Law of the Sea: Official Records, 2nd Session, Caracas, 20 June-29 August 1974 (New York: United Nations, 1975).

World Coast Conference, convened by the World Bank, 1-5 November 1993, Noordwijk, The Netherlands (includes the Noordwijk Guidelines for Integrated Coastal Zone Management).

1.4 National legislation

Nigeria

Deep Offshore and Inland Basin Production Sharing Contracts, Decree No 9 of 1999, as amended. Laws of the Federation of Nigeria, http://www.nigeria-law.org/DeepOffshoreAndInlandBasinProductionSharingContractsDecree1999.htm.

United States

Outer Continental Shelf Lands Act, 43 U.S.C. § 1331 et seq.; 43 U.S.C. § 1801 et seq.
Deep Water Royalty Relief Act, 30 CFR Part 203.

2. SECONDARY MATERIALS

2.1 Literature

Bouwer, Laurens M. and Jeroen C. J. H. Aerts, "Financing Climate Change Adaptation," 30(1) *Disasters* 49–63 (2006).

Carrera, Galo, "Geographical Scope and Scientific Challenges posed by Article 76 to the United Nations Convention on the Law of the Sea." Paper presented at UNCLOS and the Delineation of the Continental Shelf: Opportunities and Challenges to States, a Commission on the Continental Shelf Open Meeting, Seventh Session, Trusteeship Council, UN Headquarters, New York, 1 May 2000.

Chircop, Aldo. "Energy Policy and International Royalty: A Dormant Servitude Relevant for Offshore Development." In Myron H. Nordquist, John Norton Moore and Alexander Skaridov, eds., *International Energy Policy, the Arctic and the Law of the Sea* (Leiden/ Boston: Martinus Nijhoff, 2005), 247-270.

Chircop, Aldo, "Operationalizing Article 82 of the United Nations Convention on the Law of the Sea: A New Role for the International Seabed Authority?" 18 *Ocean Yb* 395-412 (2004).

Chircop, Aldo and Bruce Marchand, "International Royalty and Continental Shelf Limits: Emerging Issues for the Canadian Offshore," 26(2) *Dal. L. J.* 273-302 (Fall 2003).

Chircop, Aldo and Bruce Marchand, "Oceans Act: Uncharted Seas for Offshore Development in Atlantic Canada?" 24 *Dal. L. J.* 23-50 (2001).

Cicin-Sain, Biliana and Robert Knecht, *Integrated Coastal and Ocean Management: Concepts and Practices* (Washington, D.C.: Island Press, 1998).

Croker, Peter, "The Mandate and Work of the Commission on the Limits of the Continental Shelf," paper presented at UNCLOS and the Delineation of the Continental Shelf: Opportunities and Challenges to States, a Commission on the Continental Shelf Open Meeting, Seventh Session, Trusteeship Council, UN Headquarters, New York, 1 May 2000.

Dupuy, R. J. and D. Vignes, *A Handbook on the New Law of the Sea* (The Hague: Nijhoff, 1991), 375-381.

"International Unitization of Oil and Gas Fields: the Legal Framework of International Law, National Laws, and Private Contracts." 2 *O.G.E.L.J.* (2007).

International Maritime Boundaries vols. I-V (Leiden: Brill, 1993-2005):
———— Vols. I & II: Jonathan I. Charney and Lewis M. Alexander, eds. (1993)
———— Vol. III: Jonathan I. Charney and Lewis M. Alexander, eds. (1998)
———— Vol. IV: Jonathan I. Charney and Robert W. Smith, eds. (2002)
———— Vol. V: David A. Colson and Robert W. Smith, eds. (2005)

International Law Association (Committee on the Outer Continental Shelf), "Report on Article 82 of the UN Convention on the Law of the Sea (UNCLOS)," Rio De Janeiro Conference, 2008, http://www.ila-hq.org/en/committees/index.cfm/cid/33.

International Oil Pollution Compensation Funds: Annual Report 2002 (London: IOPCF, 2002).

International Oil Pollution Compensation Funds: Annual Report 2007 (London: IOPCF, 2007), http://www.iopcfund.org/AR07_E.pdf.

Koh, Tommy T. B., "A Constitution for the Oceans," in *The Law of the Sea: Compendium of Basic Documents* (Kingston, Jamaica: International Seabed Authority and Caribbean Law Publishing Co., 2001), lx-lxiv.

Kramer, Bruce M. and Owen L. Andersen, "The Rule of Capture: An Oil and Gas Perspective," 35 *Env. L.* 899-954 (2005).

Lang Weaver, J. and David Asmus, "Unitizing Oil and Gas Fields Around the World: A Comparative Analysis of National Laws and Private Contracts," 28 (3) *Houst. J.I.L.* (2006), http://papers.ssrn.com/sol3/papers.cfm?abstract_id=900645.

Lodge, Michael W., "The International Seabed Authority and Article 82 of the United Nations Convention on the Law of the Sea," 21(3) *Int. J. Mar. & Coast. L.* 323-333 (2006).

Lodge, Michael W., "The International Seabed Authority: Its Future Directions," in Myron H. Nordquist, John Norton Moore and Tomas H. Heidar, eds., *Legal and Scientific Aspects of Continental Shelf Limits* (Leiden: Brill, 2004), 403-409.

McNair (Lord), *The Law of Treaties* (Oxford: Clarendon Press, 1961).

Mingay, George, "Article 82 of the LOS Convention – Revenue Sharing – The Mining Industry's Perspective," 21 *Int. J. of Mar. & Coast. L.* 335-346 (2006).

Murton Bramley J., Lindsay M. Parsons, Peter Hunter and Peter Miles, *Global Non-Living Resources on the Extended Continental Shelf: Prospects at the Year 2000*, Technical Study: No.1 (Kingston: International Seabed Authority, 2001).

Nandan, Satya N. and Shabtai Rosenne, vol. eds., *United Nations Convention on the Law of the Sea 1982: A Commentary*, Vol. 2 (Dordrecht: Martinus Nijhoff Publishers, 1993).

Nardo, M., M. Saisana, A. Saltelli, Stefano Tarantola, Andres Hoffman and Enrico Giovannini, *Handbook on Constructing Composite Indicators: Methodology and User Guide,* OECD Statistics Working Paper (Paris: OECD, Statistics Directorate, 2005).

Non-living and living resources of the seafloor beyond 200 nautical miles and their significance for application of Article 82 of the United Nations Convention on the Law of the Sea, ISA Technical study no. 5 (Kingston, Jamaica: International Seabed Authority, 2009).

Nordquist, Myron H. and Choon-ho Park, eds., *Reports of the United States Delegation to the Third United Nations Conference on the Law of the Sea* (Honolulu: Law of the Sea Institute, 1983).

Nordquist, Myron H., S. Rosenne and L.B. Sohn, vol. eds., *United Nations Convention on the Law of the Sea 1982: A Commentary*, Vol. V (Dordrecht: Nijhoff, 1989).

Ong, David M., "Joint Development of Common Offshore Oil and Gas Deposits: 'Mere' State Practice or Customary International Law?" 93 *A.J.I.L.* 771 (1999).

Ong, David M., "A Legal Regime for the Outer Continental Shelf? An Inquiry as to the Rights and Duties of Coastal States within the Outer Continental Shelf," paper presented at ABLOS Tutorials and Conference, Addressing Difficult Issues in UNCLOS, Monaco, 28-30 October 2003, http://www.gmat.unsw.edu.au/ablos/ABLOS03Folder/PAPER7-4.PDF.

Pardo, Arvid, *The Common Heritage: Selected Papers on Oceans and World Order 1967-1974* (Malta: Malta University Press, 1975).

Payoyo, Peter Bautista, *Cries of the Sea: World Inequality, Sustainable Development and the Common Heritage of Humanity* (Leiden: Nijhoff, 1997).

Pettie, Alan, T., "Are Royalty Agreements Required for Canada East Coast Offshore Oil and Gas?" (2001) 24 *Dal. L. J.* 151.

Richardson, G. Ed, et al., *Deepwater Gulf of Mexico 2008: America's Offshore Energy Future*, Minerals Management Service, OCS Report 2008-013, http://www.gomr.mms.gov/PDFs/2008/2008-013.pdf.

Roughton, Dominic, "The Rights (and Wrongs) of Capture: International Law and the Implications of the Guyana/Suriname Arbitration" (Tokyo: Herbert Smith LLP in association with Gleiss Lutz and Stibbe, undated).

United Nations Development Programme, *Measuring Human Development: A Primer* (New York: UNDP, 2007), http://hdr.undp.org/en/media/Primer_complete.pdf.

Woodliffe, J.C., "International Unitization of an Offshore Gas Field." 26 *I.C.L.Q.* 338-353 (1977).

2.2 News reports

"C-NLOPB receives 5 exploration bids offshore Newfoundland, Labrador," C-NLOPB 17 November 2008, http://www.rigzone.com/news/article.asp?a_id=69563.

"Eni makes new oil discovery offshore Angola," Reuters Africa, 14 October 2008, http://africa.reuters.com/business/news/usnJOE49D0AB.html.

"Eni starts ball rolling on new Angolan project," 10(21) *Deepwater International* 1 (20 October 2008).

"Offshore drilling to take years to commence after expiration of ban," The Ledger.Com, http://www.theledger.com/article/20080925/news/809250388.

"Play potential in the deepwater Santos Basin," 68(9) *Offshore* (September 2008), http://www.offshore-mag.com/display_article/272394/120/ARTCL/none/none/1/Play-potential-in-the-deepwater-Santos-basin,-Brazil/.

"Seabed Assembly Discusses Secretary-General's Annual Report," ISA Press Release, SB/9/12, 5 August 2003.

"West Africa shows promise," 68(5) *Offshore* (1 May 2008), http://www.offshore-mag.com/articles/save_screen.cfm?ARTICLE_ID=329197.

2.3 Websites

Association of International Petroleum Negotiators (AIPN), http://www.aipn.org/modelagreements/.

Canada-Newfoundland and Labrador Offshore Petroleum Board (C-NOPB), http://www.cnlopb.nl.ca/.

Commission on the Limits of the Continental Shelf, http://www.un.org/Depts/los/clcs_new/clcs_home.htm.

International Oil Pollution Compensation Funds, http://www.iopcfund.org/.

International Seabed Authority, http://www.isa.org.jm/.

United Nations Development Programme, Human Development Report, http://hdr.undp.org/.

United Nations, Division for Oceans Affairs and the Law of the Sea, http://www.un.org/Depts/los/index.htm.

United Nations Department of Economic and Social Affairs, Division for Sustainable Development, http://www.un.org/esa/sustdev.

United Nations Framework Convention on Climate Change, http://unfccc.int/2860.php.

United Nations Treaty Collection, http://treaties.un.org/Pages/Home.aspx?lang=en.

United States Department of the Interior, Minerals Management Service (Gulf of Mexico Region), http://www.gomr.mms.gov/.

United States Energy Information Administration, http://www.eia.doe.gov/oil_gas/natural_gas/analysis_publications/ngmajorleg/continental.html.

United States Senate Committee on Foreign Relations' Hearing on the United Nations Convention on the Law of the Sea, Washington, D.C., 21 October 2003. http://foreign.senate.gov/hearings/2003/hrg031021a.html.

World Bank, http://web.worldbank.org/.

2.4 Other

A Modern Chinese-English Dictionary (Beijing: Foreign Language Teaching and Research Press, 2001).

Black's Law Dictionary, 8th ed. (St. Paul, MN: Thomson/West, 2005).

Guillen, Raymond and Jean Vincent, *Lexique de termes juridiques* (Paris: Dalloz, 1988).

Le petit Robert, (Paris: Dictionnaires Le Robert, 2002).

Oxford English Dictionary, Comp. Ed. (Oxford: Oxford University Press, 1971; 26th US Printing).

The Pinyin Chinese-English Dictionary (Beijing: Foreign Languages Institute, 1985).

www.ingramcontent.com/pod-product-compliance
Lightning Source LLC
Chambersburg PA
CBHW060621210326
41520CB00010B/1423